THE EXHORTATION TO PHILOSOPHY

IAMBLICHUS:

The Exhortation to Philosophy

INCLUDING THE LETTERS OF IAMBLICHUS
AND
PROCLUS' COMMENTARY ON THE
CHALDEAN ORACLES

TRANSLATED FROM THE GREEK BY
THOMAS MOORE JOHNSON

WITH A FOREWORD BY
JOSCELYN GODWIN

EDITED BY STEPHEN NEUVILLE

PHANES PRESS
1988

To my wife, Alice H. Johnson, I dedicate this work as a token of admiration and love.

© 1988 by Phanes Press

95 94 93 92 91 90 89 88   4 3 2 1

Published by Phanes Press, PO Box 6114, Grand Rapids, MI 49516, USA.

This book is printed on alkaline paper which conforms to the permanent paper standard developed by the National Information Standards Organization.

Library of Congress Cataloging-in-Publication Data

Iamblichus, fl. ca. 250-ca. 330.
    The exhortation to philosophy.

    Translation of: Exhortation to philosophy.
    1. Philosophy—Early works to 1800. I. Proclus, ca. 410-485. Chaldean oracles. English. 1988. II. Neuville, Stephen. III. Title.
B669.E922E5   1988   186'.4   88-29003
ISBN 0-933999-62-3 (alk. paper)
ISBN 0-933999-63-1 (pbk.: alk. paper)

Printed and bound in the United States of America.

CONTENTS

FOREWORD

In a little stone house overlooking the river Osage, a Midwestern lawyer sits among his eight thousand books and escapes for a while into the world of the Ideal. He is one of the chosen few on whom the Spirit of Plato has descended, demanding a lifetime's devotion to the philosophy that is also a religion. The universities have spurned him because he does not have a German doctorate. The local people of Osceola, Missouri, think him strange and aloof: a lawyer without ambition, who only leaves home to fetch more books from the post office. Once he tried to run a philosophy club in town, but after a while he realized that he was the only philosopher there. In the 1880s, whenever funds allowed, he put out a magazine, *The Platonist*. Now, in 1907, he breaks a silence of seventeen years with this translation of Iamblichus' *Exhortation to Philosophy*.

Thomas Moore Johnson (1851-1919) was only 22 when he wrote to Bronson Alcott, the Platonist of Concord, Mass., saying modestly that "After a diligent study of Plotinus, Proclus, Julian, Taylor, etc., etc., I consider myself qualified to explain the dogmas of Plato and his disciples."[1] Their correspondence continued for years, and indeed it was his network of correspondents, rather than personal contacts, that kept Johnson going. The life of a modern Platonist is bound to be a lonely one, for he can expect no empathy either from his neighbors, devotees of quite other idols, nor from the learned of the universities, for whom Platonism is not a religion but one philosophy among others. The life of the English Platonist Thomas Taylor (1758-1835) had been no more successful in worldly terms, yet the sprouting of Platonists in unlikely corners such as Osceola, Missouri, Jacksonville and Quincy, Indiana—even Grand Rapids, Michigan—was largely due to Taylor's immense labors of transla-

---

1) See Kathleen Raine and George Mills Harper, eds., *Thomas Taylor the Platonist: Selected Writings*, Princeton University Press, 1969, p. 74.

tion.[2] Johnson followed consciously in Taylor's footsteps with a program of study, translation, and commentary, so as to put the works of the "Platonic Succession" into the hands of the few who would value them as he did.

The original author of this work, Iamblichus of Chalcis, was a pupil of Porphyry, who had been a pupil of Plotinus; but here he looks rather to the fountain-head, to Aristotle and to Plato himself. The *Exhortation to Philosophy* evidently arose from a course of introductory lectures at Iamblichus' school, and is a digest made for an audience who did not have our easy access to copies of the originals. It is interesting to see how Iamblichus reduces the immensity of Plato's and Aristotle's thought to manageable proportions. He turns to Plato's *Phædo* for the arguments in favor of the philosophic life, and to the *Republic* for what are perhaps the most telling of all Plato's myths: that of the Sun, and the famous allegory of the Cave. Iamblichus' use of Aristotle shows that he does not regard him as the rival of Plato, but as a fellow philosopher who wrote in the *Nicomachean Ethics* of contemplation as the highest goal of human existence. Moreover, he preserves for us what are probably extensive passages of Aristotle's lost *Protrepticus*, likewise a plea for a life based on philosophy.[3]

One of the most valuable aspects of this book is its most unfashionable one: the tone of extreme Platonic dogmatism, designed to make converts for the movement. Some Iamblichus hopes to win through logical argument and syllogism, others through fear of the consequences of an unphilosophic life. (At the same time, the Christians were vying for the same souls, using similar stratagems.) Few readers are likely to share Iamblichus' attitude to the body and the material world, here blandly opposed as "evil" to the "good" of the immaterial world to which philosophy (or Christianity) gives access; Plato and Aristotle, certainly, were more subtle than that. When our philosopher extends the same moralizing

---

2) See Paul R. Anderson, *Platonism in the Midwest*, New York, Columbia University Press, for Temple University Publications, 1963, including the best published account of Thomas Johnson, pp. 151-185.

3) See Ingemar Düring, *Aristotle's Protrepticus: An Attempt at Reconstruction*, Göteborg University, 1961.

dualism to the sexes, I must confess to being on the side of the "bright and lively Thracian girl" who laughed when Thales fell into the well (see page 70); and when he praises the philosopher's incompetence in worldly matters, I recall unkindly that Iamblichus could well afford to despise worldly goods, since he himself owned slaves and several "suburban villas."[4]

But if Iamblichus seems narrow-minded, we moderns are no less shackled by the obligatory dogmas of our own time. The world-view that is taken for granted today is as unphilosophic as it could possibly be, and to cure it needs a strong medicine. It is salutary to be reminded of that, by pressure on the opposite end of the scale.

More than that, there is something here that transcends the fashions of both our epochs, speaking to us post-Freudians, post-Marxists, and very likely post-Christians as it spoke to the equally confused and neurotic souls of the third century. It is the exhortation to add a further dimension to our lives, and one which is infinitely rich. For the earth and our existence on it are limited: however important they may be in their own right, there is that Other to which part of us also belongs, which knows no limitation whatsoever. In embracing a philosophy worthy of the name, we prepare for our entry into that.

In the end, what Iamblichus seems to mean by the practice of philosophy is nothing more or less than what we would call meditation; and the advice one gains from careful reading is to meditate by withdrawing one's attention from everything but the Absolute. The challenge to philosophers in our time is to pursue this goal without joining Iamblichus in his contempt for the here and now. No doubt it was a daily challenge to Thomas Johnson himself, when he left the philosophic calm of his riverside book-house and returned to the wife and three sons who were awaiting him in the world which, to them, was equally real.

—JOSCELYN GODWIN

---

4) Eunapius, *Lifes of the Philosophers*, 458.

INTRODUCTION

The English language, by reason of the poverty of its philosophical vocabulary, is inadequate to fully express the deep insights of the Platonic thinkers. Their books are in a "sealed dialect" to the many, in any language, and to the mere verbal Greek scholar as well as to those who are innocent of Greek they are unintelligible. Chemistry, Biology, and the other natural "sciences" have technical vocabularies, and Philosophy, the Science of sciences, has a vocabulary peculiar to itself, and this must be mastered before one can apprehend philosophic conceptions. Philology alone will not furnish a key to the thought of Plato and the Platonists. Plotinus, having read the treatise of Longinus, the famous critic, *On Principles*, observed that Longinus "was indeed a philologist but by no means a philosopher." Longinus himself, a man of the widest literary culture, acknowledged that he could not understand many of the hypotheses of the books of Plotinus, but this did not prevent him from holding in the highest esteem the philosophy of that mighty thinker. Contrary to the custom of modern critics, he did not condemn what he did not understand, merely because he did not understand it. Porson, probably the greatest verbal Greek scholar of modern times, said that Plutarch, whose conceptions are comparatively easy to grasp, was "too much for him." Of course the mere grammatical interpretation of the language of Plutarch was as easy to Porson as the reading of an English book, but he recognized his incapacity to deal with the concepts of Philosophy. But the average Ph.D. of this generation lacks Porson's candor. He is conceited enough to fancy that he is competent, without any other qualification than a philological knowledge of the Greek, and even that often of the scantiest form, not only to understand but even to criticize the writings of the Platonists. The effrontery of ignorance could hardly go further. More, much more, is required for the apprehension of Platonic ideas than a grammatical acquaintance with the Greek language. Many of the efforts of mere philologists to explain the doctrines and analyze the language of the Platonic philosophers are absolutely ludicrous. Dissertations "for the doctor's degree" have appeared which, given a knowledge of the Greek alphabet and the ability to count, were not beyond the capacity of a ten year old school child. Dr. W.T. Harris, unquestionably the profoundest thinker of this country, well exposes the absurdity of the complaint, made by ignorant or indolent persons, about the alleged difficulties of the philosophic language: "the crusade against technical words continues still. People are frequently saying: 'if you would only give your thoughts in common language it would be so much easier to understand you.' With all seriousness, these people are radically mistaken. If speculative thoughts were crowded into 'common language,' they would of course appear like common thoughts, if the expression means anything. *For what is wanted is easily comprehended thoughts.* Now suppose a deep and true thought were so expressed, in common language, as to seem a trite remark or a truism: commonplace thinkers would slide over it smoothly, and see no deep thought at all, while a few deep thinkers, on the alert, might catch the subtle under-meaning. If, on the contrary, the thought preserves a technical expression, the easy, common-place thinker receives a severe shock when he comes upon it, and is not left in a state of doubt whether he understands it or not. He sees at once that he does not "make sense" of it. If he is simple and sincere, and withal possessed of humility, he will summon his powers, and, by hard thinking, master the passage. He will be rewarded by the consciousness of added power which increased insight gives. But if he is conceited and vain, it is likely that he will accuse the author of obscurity and confusion of thoughts."[1]

Every translation from the Greek is more or less defective and unsatisfactory, and the version of Iamblichus' *Exhortation to the Study of Philosophy* now printed will not be found an exception to the rule. I have simply aimed to reproduce faithfully in English the manner and thought of the original text, but to what extent this has

1) *Journal of Speculative Philosophy,* vol. 5, p. 280.

been done must be determined by others. It would be a severe and just reflection on this translation if it could be truly said of it that it read like an original work. No accurate translation, by reason of its very nature, ought to resemble an original production. The reader is entitled to have the manner as well as the matter of an ancient author presented to him. In other words, a faithful translation will show not only *what* the original writer said, but *how* he said it. This translation is not intended for the Greek scholar, who will read the writings of Iamblichus in the original, if at all—but it was made and is printed for the benefit of those who, ignorant of Greek, ardently desire to acquire a knowledge of Platonic thought. The work was not designed for the proficient in Philosophy: it is avowedly of an elementary character, though by no means lacking in profound thoughts and insights. Compared with many modern "philosophical" books now enjoying an ephemeral popularity, it may well and truly be termed 'profound.' All lovers of perennial wisdom who are Greek scholars are urged to read and study the original text of the writings of Plato and his genuine interpreters, wherein they will find an inexhaustible store of intellectual knowledge of the loftiest type; and all who are not Greek scholars are advised to master the Greek language, because it is the key to intellectual treasures far more precious than all the material wealth of the world. The time and labor necessary to master the Greek, the most perfect instrument of thought ever given by Divinity to mankind, and the shrine of the most sublime wisdom, could not possibly be more profitably expended. "To be competently skilled in ancient learning is by no means of such insuperable pains. The very progress itself is attended with delight, and resembles a journey through some pleasant country, where every mile we advance new charms arise. It is certainly as easy to be a scholar as a gamester, or any other characters equally illiberal and low. The same application, the same quantity of habit, will fit us for one as completely as for the other. And as to those who tell us, with an air of seeming wisdom, that *it is men* and *not books* we must study to become knowing,—this I have always remarked, from repeated experience, to be the common consolation and language of dunces."[2] True, a knowledge of Greek is not indispensable for the apprehension of Ancient Thought, but for obvious reasons it is certainly better to study it in the original texts of its exponents rather than in translations, good, bad, or indifferent.

In producing this work I have used freely the various translations of Plato, but chiefly those of Taylor, Cope, and Davies & Vaughan. Their text, however, I have not hesitated to change, whenever I thought that the rendering could be improved. The notes to Dr. Adam's edition of the *Republic* have been of much assistance. I am specially indebted to Prof. Ingram Bywater's paper, "On a Lost Dialogue of Aristotle "[3] and Mr. Thomas Whittaker's *The Neoplatonists*, the best modern work on the subject which has appeared: his abstract of the *Exhortation* I have found very helpful.

The text of Iamblichus is in a corrupt condition. Some of the corrupt passages are easy to emend, the sense and structure of the text clearly showing what is demanded, but others are beyond correction. Iamblichus, moreover, is a difficult author to interpret. The changes of pronouns, the long and involved sentences, the abrupt beginnings and endings, all these and other idiosyncrasies are in the original, and must re-appear, partially at least, in the translation. Steadily intent on the formulation and expression of his thought, Iamblichus gave little or no heed to his style. Hence, as Eunapius says, he does not detain the reader nor invite him to the perusal of his works by the beauty of his style, but rather repels him. But the critic of his manner must remember that, owing to the gross carelessness of transcribers, there are many blunders and obscurities in his books for which he was not responsible.

I could not avail myself of any prior English version of the *Exhortation* as a whole, because none has been published; but Stanley in his *History of Philosophy* (London, 1655) and Bridgman (London, 1804) translated the last chapter, which contains an

2) *Hermes*, by James Harris.

3) *Journal of Philology*, vol. 2. Professor Bywater, Regius Professor of Greek in the University of Oxford, is one of the very best Greek scholars in England, or elsewhere. The notes to his admirable edition of Priscianus Lydus enable one to recover much of Iamblichus' treatise On the Soul which was largely used by Prisciannus. Certainly, as Professor Bywater says, Iamblichus "makes no secret of the composite origin of his book," but, nevertheless, there is much more originality in the Exhortation than is generally supposed.

explanation of the Pythagoric Symbols. These versions have been utilized. The fragments of Archytas, cited by Iamblichus in the third chapter, and certain "Pythagoric Sentences," were translated by Thomas Taylor the Platonist, and printed in his version of Iamblichus' *Life of Pythagoras*. These I have revised and used. To Taylor, easily the greatest and most thorough of modern Platonists, all students of the Platonic Philosophy are under innumerable obligations. His audacious avowal that he was a "perfect convert" to the Heathen religion in every particular, "so far as it was understood and illustrated by the Pythagoric and Platonic philosophers," aroused against him the ire of the ecclesiastics of his age, who denounced him savagely; and the verbal Greek scholars of the time, who were mostly ecclesiastics, or under ecclesiastical influence, charged him with ignorance of Greek, though he knew more of the genius and meaning of the Greek language than the whole crowd of his enemies and critics. This is true despite the fact that he made some blunders in his numerous translations, caused chiefly by the haste with which he worked.

It would be unjust, in this connection, to pass without notice Mr. G.R.S. Mead's indefatigable labors in behalf of the dissemination of ancient thought. It was at his instance that the reprints of Taylor's translations of Iamblichus' *On the Mysteries* and other Platonic works were made, and he contributed to *Lucifer* a series of valuable and appreciative articles on the "Lives of the Later Platonists." His last work—*Thrice-Greatest Hermes*—containing a translation of the extant sermons and fragments of the Trismegistic Literature, may be heartily recommended to every student of the wisdom of the Ancients.

Life and Writings of Iamblichus

Iamblichus was "born" at Chalcis, in Syria, about 260 A.D., and "died" about 330. He consecrated his life to the services of Philosophy, spending his time in contemplation, teaching and writing: his disciples were numerous, and his fame as a teacher and thinker was great and widely-diffused. "It is well known to every tyro in Platonism that he was dignified by all the Platonists that succeeded him with the epithet of *divine;* and after the encomium passed on him by the acute Emperor Julian, 'that he was posterior indeed in time but not in genius to Plato,' all further praise of him would be as unnecessary, as the defamation of him by certain modern critics is contemptible and idle. For these *homunculi,* looking solely to his deficiency in point of style and not to the magnitude of his intellect, perceive only his little blemishes, but have not even a glimpse of his surpassing excellence."[4]

I. *De Mysteriis Aegyptiorum, Chaldaeorum, Assyriorum:* On the Mysteries of the Egyptians, Chaldeans and Assyrians. Edited by Parthey, Greek and Latin, Berlin, 1857. Translated by Thomas Taylor, London, 1821; second edition, London, 1895. A new translation by Prof. Alexander Wilder appeared in *The Platonist,* and a thorough revision of this version is now in manuscript. This famous work is of the greatest value to all students of ancient lore, and "is the most copious, the clearest, and the most satisfactory defense extant of genuine ancient theology."

II. *De Secta Pythagorica:* On the Pythagorean School. This treatise was in ten books, of which only five are extant. 1. *De Vita Pythagorica Liber:* On the Pythagoric Life, or Life of Pythagoras. Edited by Nauck, St. Petersburg, 1884. Translated by Thomas Taylor, London, 1818. "A most interesting work; and the benefits are inestimable, which the dissemination of it is calculated to produce." 2. *Adhortatio ad Philosophiam:* Exhortation to the Study of Philosophy. Edited by Pistelli, Leipzig, 1888. English translation in this volume. 3. *De Communi Mathematica Scientia:* On the Common Mathematical Science. Edited by Festa, Leipzig, 1891. "He who reads and understands this admirable work will clearly perceive the essence, power, and energies of the whole of the mathematical science; what the common speculation of it is, and to what genera it is extended; what the principles of the mathematical sciences are, and in what they differ from other principles; what the nature is of the principles of other essences, and how principles of this kind impart a common cause to all the mathematical sciences, etc.... All this, and still more than this, the reader may learn from this invaluable work." The fact that there is no English version of

4) Thomas Taylor.

this book is a special argument for the reader to learn Greek. 4. *Commentarius in Nicomachi Arithmeticam Introductionem:* Commentary on Nicomachus' *Introduction to Arithmetic.* Edited by Pistelli, Leipzig, 1894. Taylor's *Theoretic Arithmetic* contains "the substance of all that has been written on this subject by Theon of Smyrna, Nicomachus, Iamblichus, and Boethius." 5-6-7. *De Physicis, Ethicis, et Divinis quae in Numerorum Doctrina Observantur:* On the Natural, Ethical and Divine Conceptions which are Perceived in the Science of Numbers. Of these only the seventh, the *Theologumena Arithmeticae,* or Theological Speculations on Arithmetic, is extant. Edited by Ast, Leipzig, 1817. 8. *Institutiones Musicae ad Mentem Pythagoreorum.* Lost. 9. *Institutiones Geometricae ad Mentem Pythagoreorum.* Lost. 10. *Institutiones Sphericae ad Mentem Pythagoreorum.* Lost.

III. *De Divinitate Imaginum Liber:* On the Divinity of Images. Only fragments remain.

IV. *Epistolae ad Aretem, Macedonium, Sopatrem, Asphalium,* etc. Many fragments of the Letters are preserved by Stobaeus.

V. *De Diis:* Concerning the Gods. Lost. "From this work the Emperor Julian derived most of the dogmata contained in his elegant 'Oration to the Sovereign Sun.' "

VI. Commentaries on the *Parmenides*, *Timaeus* and *Phaedo* of Plato. Lost. "The inestimable value of the first and second of these Commentaries is sufficiently evident from the frequent mention made of them by Proclus in his writings on these dialogues; and from the admirable passages in them which he has fortunately preserved." Olympiodorus' quotations from the *Commentary on the Phaedo* plainly prove that it is equal in value to the others.

VII. *Concerning the Perfection of the Chaldaic Philosophy.* Lost. "The twenty-seventh book of this great work is cited by Damascius in his treatise *On First Principles*, and this whole discourse was studied with avidity by Proclus, and enabled him, as we are informed by Marinus, to ascend to the very summit of theurgic virtue."

VIII. Commentaries on the *Categories* and *Prior Analytics* of Aristotle. Lost.

IX. *De Anima:* On the Soul. Fragments have been preserved by

Stobæus, and Priscianus Lydus, in his *Commentary on Theophrastus*. Simplicius, in his *Commentary on the* de Anima *of Aristotle*, often cites this treatise of Iamblichus.

X. *Monobiblon:* a book showing that the transmigrations of souls are not from men to irrational animals, nor from irrational animals to men, but from animals to animals, and from men to men. Lost. Quoted by Nemesius *De Natura Hominis*, ii, 7.

XI. *Alypii Vita:* Life of Alypius. Lost.

XII. Treatise On the Best Judgment. Lost. Cited by Syrianus in his *Commentary on Hermogenes*.

XIII. *In Platonis Dialogos Commentariorum Fragmenta*: Fragments of the Commentaries on Plato's Dialogues. Edited with translation and commentary by J.M. Dillon, Leiden, 1973.

Every word written by Iamblichus is highly prized by all who desire to gain more than a superficial knowledge of the Platonic system. The fragments of his letters are replete with insights richly worthy of apprehension.

The Excerpts from Proclus' *Commentary on the Chaldean Oracles*, short as they are, will be found most interesting by all who are devoted to abstruse research. The best edition of the Oracles is that by Thomas Taylor in the *Classical Journal,* vols. XVI and XVII, London, 1818. Kroll's work, *De Oraculis Chaldaicis* (Breslau, 1894) contains much good material, but he has no conception of the deep philosophy involved in the Oracles. Jahn's *Commentarius* and *Glossarium ad Oracula Chaldaica* are of great aid in elucidating the meaning of the Chaldaic Vocabulary.

—THOMAS M. JOHNSON
OSCEOLA, MISSOURI, JUNE 18, 1907

THE EXHORTATION TO PHILOSOPHY

1. Of Pythagoras and the life in accordance with his doctrines, and of the Pythagoreans, we treated sufficiently in our first book:[1] we will now explain the remaining part of his system, beginning with the common preparatory training prescribed by his school in reference to all education and learning and virtue; a training which is not partial, only perfecting one in some particular good of all these but which, to speak simply, incites his cognitive powers to the acquirement of all disciplines, all sciences, all beautiful and noble actions in life, all species of culture—and, in a phrase, every thing which participates in the Beautiful. For without an awakening, caused by exhortation, from the natural lethargy, it is not possible for one to apply himself suddenly to beautiful and noble studies; nor can one immediately proceed to the apprehension of the highest and most perfect good before his soul has been duly prepared by exhortation, [which arouses his impulses to higher things, purifies his thoughts, and directs his actions].

But just as the soul gradually advances to the greater from the less, passing through all beautiful things, and finally reaches the most perfect goods, so it is necessary that exhortation should proceed regularly, beginning from those things which are common. For exhortation will incite to Philosophy itself and to philosophizing in general, according to every system of thought, no particular school being expressly preferred, but all being approved according to their respective merits, and ranked higher than mere human studies, by a common and popular mode of exhorting. After this we must use a mediate method which, though neither entirely popular nor Pythagorean, is not wholly distinct from either of these modes. In this mediate course we will arrange the exhortations common to

---

1) Iamblichus is referring to his *Life of Pythagoras*, contained in The *Pythagorean Sourcebook and Library: An Anthology of Ancient Writings which Relate to Pythagoras and Pythagorean Philosophy*, Grand Rapids, Phanes Press, 1987.

all philosophy, which are not deduced from the Pythagorean teaching and are therefore different from it; but we will add the most suitable and characteristic opinions of the Pythagoreans, in order that there may be a Pythagorean exhortation according to this mediate mode of discoursing. After this we will gradually, as is reasonable, depart from the exoteric conceptions and pass to and become familiar with the special and technical demonstrations of the Pythagorean school, ascending by means of these as by a sort of bridge or ladder as it were from a depth to a great height. And, lastly, we will interpret the exhortations characteristic of the Pythagorean school, which are strange and mystical in a certain respect, if they are considered in relation to other systems of philosophic culture.

II. We will begin from those things which for our instruction are primary. These are perspicuous and evident to all, and though they do not apprehend the power and essence of Virtue, yet according to common conceptions about Virtue they awaken our desire for good through certain aphorisms which are familiar to many and are expressed in accordance with the visible images of real beings. These are thus set forth:

(1) As we live through the soul, it must be said that by the virtue of this we live well; just as, since we see through the eyes, it is by virtue of these that we see well.

(2) It must not be thought that gold can be injured by rust, or virtue tainted by baseness.

(3) We should betake ourselves to virtue as to an inviolable temple, in order that we may not be exposed to any ignoble insolence of the irrational element of the soul.

(4) We should confide in virtue as in a chaste wife, but trust Fortune as we would a fickle mistress.

(5) It is better that virtue should be received with poverty, than wealth with vice; and frugality with health, than abundance with disease.

(6) As much food is injurious to the body, so is much wealth pernicious to the soul evilly inclined or disposed.

(7) It is equally dangerous to give a sword to a madman, and power to a depraved man.

(8) Just as it is better for a purulent part of the body to be burned than to remain diseased, so it is also better for a depraved man to die than to live.

(9) The theorems of Philosophy are to be enjoyed as much as possible, as if they were ambrosia and nectar; for the pleasure arising from them is genuine, incorruptible and divine. Magnanimity they are also able to produce, and though they cannot make us eternal beings, yet they enable us to obtain a scientific knowledge of eternal natures.

(10) If vigor of the senses is desirable, much more should prudence be sought; for it is as it were the sensitive vigor of our practical intellect. And as by the former we are protected from deception in sensations, so through the latter we avoid false reasoning in practical affairs.

(11) We shall worship the Deity rightly if we render our intellect pure from all vice, as from some kind of stain or disgrace.

(12) We should adorn a temple with gifts, but the soul with disciplines.

(13) As prior to the greater mysteries the lesser are delivered, so a disciplinary training must precede the study and acquisition of Philosophy.

(14) The fruits of the earth are indeed annually imparted, but the fruits of Philosophy at every season of the year.

(15) Just as land must be specially cultivated by him who wishes to obtain from it the best fruit, so the soul should be most carefully and attentively cultivated, in order that it may produce fruit worthy its nature.

If anyone should contribute additional aphoristic similitudes of this kind, drawn from things manifest to all, he will by a common reason arouse students to the study of Philosophy.

III. There is another form of exhortative instruction which uses maxims—no longer by comparison contrasting different similitudes—which is metrical and harmonious, and genuinely peculiar

to Pythagoreans, examples of which are given to us in the Golden
Verses themselves and in other poems,[2] of which I will give a few
specimens:

> This do, this think, to this your heart incline,
> This way will lead you to the life divine. vv. 45-46

[Do these things, meditate on these things, love these things; for
these will lead you into the way of divine virtue.]

For by these maxims the student is exhorted to all beautiful
disciplines and studies; nor must it be thought that any labors
should be spared, or any attention or care omitted, which conduce
to the acquisition of these: again, to a love and desire of beautiful
things Pythagoras arouses the student, subserving all things to the
acquisition of virtue, and not simply of any virtue, but of that
particular virtue which separates us from human nature and leads
us to the Divine Essence, and to the knowledge and possession of
the divine virtue. But he incites the student to the theoretic or
contemplative wisdom through these verses:

> These precepts having mastered, thou shalt know
> The system of the never-dying Gods
> And the dying man, and how from all the rest
> Each thing is sunder'd, and how held in one:
> And thou shalt know, as it is right thou shouldst,
> That nature everywhere is uniform,
> And so shalt neither hope for things that lie
> Beyond all hope, nor fail of any truth. vv. 49-53.

[Practicing these precepts faithfully, you will know the constitution
of the immortal Gods, and of mortal men—how far every being
extends and by what law they are bound together. You shall also
know, so far as it is lawful, that the nature which pervades the
various species of things is always uniform, so that you may not
hope what is not to be hoped, and that you may not be ignorant of

2) For a translation of The Golden Verses of Pythagoras see *The Pythagorean Sourcebook and Library*, pp. 163-165, and this volume, pp. 113-115.

anything.]

For these verses by a power than which there is nothing more admirable incite those endowed with a genuine desire for intellectual insight to the study of the theoretic or contemplative philosophy. For the knowledge of the Gods is Virtue and Wisdom and perfect Felicity, and makes us similar to the Gods; but the knowledge of men supplies human virtues and renders us skillful in the social and business affairs of life, enabling us to discriminate among these the beneficial from the injurious, and to acquire the one and avoid the other. And, in brief, it teaches us in what way human life is constituted by thought and deed. A still more admirable thing is that we are taught by this theoretic science the law by which the divine principle or entity in each of us ascends to the higher sphere without trouble and hindrance, and by what law it is bound and obstructed so that it cannot easily progress and be released from the corporeal chains. The next maxim exhorts us to acquire a knowledge of nature and the whole theory about the heaven. For the nature of heaven is always similar to itself, revolving constantly in the same circle—if one learns this, he will neither ever expect the things which should not be expected, nor will he be ignorant of any of those things which will happen through necessity.

The succeeding maxims base the exhortation on the fact that the life we lead is deliberately and voluntarily chosen by us, as:

> Man, wretched man, thou shalt be taught to know,
> Who bears within himself the inborn cause of woe. v. 54.

[Know that mortals themselves are alone the miserable authors of evils.]

For if men are the voluntary causes or principles of actions, and have the inherent power to choose the good and avoid the evil, the one not using this power is utterly unworthy of the advantages and privileges given him by nature. Pythagoras, therefore, says nothing else than this, namely, that we choose our own destiny and career in life, and that we are our own luck and good fortune, and that we procure our own felicity. He shows that that alone which is beautiful and worthy *per se* should be chosen.

Similar to the preceding are these verses:

> Unhappy race! that never yet could tell
>> How near their good and happiness they dwell.
> Deprived of sense, they neither hear nor see;
>> Fettered in vice, they seek not to be free,
> But stupid to their own sad Fate agree. vv. 55-56.

[They neither know nor perceive that their goods are near them, and but few of them know how to deliver themselves from evils.]

For that the goods are near and connate with our own soul, and of all things are most akin to us, are facts that of themselves are wonderfully exhortative; and the fact that men neither hear nor see, blinded and deafened by sense, until they are aroused from their fatal lethargy, marvelously incites us to the intellectual life, since the intellect alone sees and hears all things. The liberation from evils, indeed, which few know how to effect, exhorts us to a separation from the body and a life of the soul *per se,* or absolutely independent of corporeal conditions, which we denominate a meditation of death. And there is another mode of exhortation in succession to this, namely that drawn from the contempt of and aversion to evils. For neither is it endurable that they should, "like cylinders roll to and fro always oppressed with innumerable ills,"[3] for evil brings violence, thoughtlessness, rashness, fickleness, and especially the indefinite and disorderly, all of which it is necessary to strenuously avoid and flee.

After this comes the following:

> For native strife in ev'ry bosom reigns,
>> And secretly an impious war maintains:
> Provoke not this but let the combat cease,
>> And ev'ry yielding passion sue for peace. vv. 58-60.

[A pernicious contention is innate in men and is their constant

---

3) Verse 58.

companion and treacherously injures them, which we should by no means provoke and arouse but, obeying the dictates of Reason, avoid.]

Here he shows that there is a twofold form of human nature—one coming to us from and by reason of our 'generation' or entrance into this material world, an alien animal, which some call a many-headed beast, others some type of mortal form of life, and others the generative nature—and the other, our essential and divine nature. Here he names this alien animal the connate contention or strife, not as having an equal rank with our primary and essential life, but as a companion attached to this life. He counsels us, therefore, to discard this connate strife or companion, and to receive in exchange for it the harmonious, uniform intellectual energy, which brings good instead of injury, and instead of falling into destruction or ruin supplies a principle of salvation; and the nonessential and secondary part of human nature, which accompanies the primary, it separates from itself as alien and hostile, but assumes the principal and most perfect life which has all things from and in itself. By reason of all these things, therefore, the former deserves to be discussed most briefly, but the latter at great length. And thus an exhortation of this kind to the intellectual life is most effective. The following maxims encourage us to strive for the divine perfection and the best condition of life, by which we may commune with the Gods:

> Wouldst thou, great Jove, thou Father of Mankind,
> Reveal the Dæmon for that task assigned,
> The wretched race an end of woes would find.
> And yet be bold, O Man! divine thou art,
> And of the Gods' celestial essence part. vv. 61-63.

[O Zeus, father of mortals, you would deliver them from all evils, if you would reveal to them what kind of dæmon they use. But take courage: the race of man is divine.]

In these, therefore, there is first a most admirable exhortation to acquire the divine felicity, mingled with prayers and invocations to the Gods, and especially to their king, Zeus: second, there is a clear manifestation of the dæmon given and allotted to each of us from the Gods, by which we are again recalled to the Gods. For neither is one otherwise able to ascend to that which is essentially most divine and primary unless he uses a genius [dæmon][4] of this kind, by whom it is necessary that every lover of the Gods should be genuinely purified. To this genius we owe, first, a liberation from the evils adhering to us from generation—and, secondly, a true knowledge of the character and quality of the divine and felicitous life, by virtue of which knowledge we may ascend and behold the principal and divine race of men, received into which we will have gained the most felicitous life offered to men by the Gods. Lastly, therefore, Pythagoras exhorts to a change in the habits of the soul, and a return of the soul to the life *per se* alone, by which mode of living it is liberated from the body and from the desires and passions inherent in the body. But he speaks thus:

> Let that best reason ever hold the rein,
>> Then, if this mortal body thou forsake,
> And thy glad flight to the pure Æther take,
>> Among the Gods exalted shalt thou shine,
> Immortal, incorruptible, divine:
>> The tyrant Death securely shalt thou brave,
> And scorn the dark dominion of the grave. vv. 69-71.

[Place intuitive Intellect as the best charioteer or guide of your acts. But if, having abandoned your body, you come into the free Æther,[5] you shall be an immortal God, incorruptible, and nevermore subject to death.]

The recognition of the primacy of intellect by constituting it the best leader of the soul preserves undefiled the similitude to the Gods to which it primarily exhorts. Then, if we leave the body and pass to the ætherial region, thereby changing the human nature into the purity of the Gods and in place of the mortal choosing the

4) Used here in the sense of a guardian spirit.
5) Æther is the fifth or quintessential element which exists above the imperfections of the sub-lunary sphere.

immortal life, we by these acts are restored to the divine order and received into the divine circuit, which was our condition prior to our descent into the human form. Wherefore it clearly appears that the method of these exhortations leads us to all the species of goods and to all the forms of the better or higher life.

IV. But now let us proceed to the exposition of the esoteric and scientific exhortations. We will first consider those which, while giving information about the principal and primary essences, at the same time impel us to a theological and intellectual investigation and knowledge of these essences, and arouse us to acquire the highest type of wisdom. Archytas,[6] accordingly, in the beginning of his treatise *On Wisdom*, exhorts thus: "Wisdom as much excels in all human affairs as the sight does the other corporeal senses, intellect the soul, and the sun the stars. For the sight is the most far-darting and the most multiform of all the senses; intellect is the supreme part of the soul judging by reason and discursive knowledge what is right, and subsisting as the sight and power of the most honorable things; and the Sun is the eye and soul of things which are in nature. For through it all things become visible, are generated, and are apprehended: moreover, deriving their roots and being generated from there, they are nourished, increased, and excited by it in conjunction with sense." Here he shows very scientifically the nature and function of wisdom; and even more importantly, he then makes an exhortation to intellect and contemplation. Moreover, another good which is wonderfully effective of exhortation is supplied. For from those things which are familiar he deduces a reminder of higher, unfamiliar natures, through a clear analogy. For that sight is the most acute, subtle, and excellent of all the senses is evident to all; nor is anyone ignorant of the fact that the Sun is superior to the stars; and that intellect is the ruling principle of the soul is assumed in even common conceptions on this subject.

From these comparisons, then, he shows perspicuously and

6) Archytas (first half of the fourth century B.C.), one of the chief Pythagoreans, was a distinguished general, statesman, mathematician, philosopher, and personal friend of Plato. For more on Archytas and his fragments see *The Pythagorean Sourcebook and Library*, pp. 177-201.

scientifically the preëminence of Wisdom in relation to all human affairs, so that the truth becomes intelligible and comprehensible to those hearing arcane things in obscure speech. Moreover, from the differences of each, the knowledge of wisdom and the exhortation to it are learned. For, first, if the sight is the most far-darting and the most multiform of all the senses, so wisdom, analogously considered, apprehends the most remote things as present and comprehends within itself the forms of all beings. Second, if the intellect is the supreme part of the soul, judging by reason and discursive knowledge what is right and subsisting as the sight and power of the most honorable things, unquestionably Wisdom similarly surpasses reason and discursive knowledge and contemplates beings by simpler conceptions than these, namely by intuitive intellections; it judges good things *per se* and perfects them in itself; it is the sight of intelligibles and subsists as the power of the most divine and perfect activities. And, finally, if the Sun is the eye and soul of natural things—for through it all things become visible, are generated, and are apprehended and, deriving their roots and being generated from thence, are nourished, increased and excited by it in conjunction with sense—it is evident from these analogies that Wisdom is the eye and life of intelligible things, and supplies perception of intelligibles and being to all beings, and is the primary cause of all production in the world and of the first generation and order. And so it is with us: is there any one who, wishing to participate in the highest felicity, will not pursue with great labor and alacrity such and so great a principle, productive of so many goods?

This, then, is the exhortation arising from the dignity and supremacy of Wisdom. That which is suggested by the nature of the true man, Archytas shows in the following words:

Man was generated by far the wisest of all terrestrial animals. For he is able to contemplate the things which exist, and to obtain from all things science and wisdom. To which also it may be added, that Divinity has engraved and exhibited in him the system of universal reason, in which all the forms of things in existence are distributed, and the signification of nouns and verbs. For a place is assigned for the sounds of the voice, namely the pharynx, the mouth and the nostrils. But as man was generated the instrument of the sounds, through which nouns and verbs are signified, so likewise of the conceptions which are expressed or represented by visible things. And this appears to me to be the work for the accomplishment of which man was generated and constituted, and received organs and powers from divinity.

This mode of exhorting is assumed from the nature of man. For if man is the wisest of animals and able to contemplate the things which truly exist, it is necessary for him to strive for theological and contemplative wisdom. And if he has the power from nature of apprehending from all things science and prudence, he ought to acquire the demonstrative science and virtue of prudence as especially worthy and proper for him. In addition, since the divinity has engraved in him the system of universal reason, in which are all the forms of things and the significations of nouns and verbs—on account of these gifts it is right that he should apprehend the whole science of logic, since man is a spectator not only of those things which are signified by words but also of the thoughts expressed in beings, and in order that he might do this work he received from the Deity instruments and powers. So on this account man should aim to acquire theoretic wisdom in the whole realm of being insofar as it is real being; and in all the species of things he should learn scientifically the principles and criteria of all knowledge. Moreover, he ought to view the intellect *per se* and the purest reason or thought, and notice how many principles from it are imparted to the beautiful and good things in human life. He should also be enthusiastic in acquiring all the virtues and the mathematical sciences and other arts or pursuits which we have discussed. And thus the exhortation based on the nature of man arouses us to the acquisition of the whole of Philosophy.

Archytas also introduces another composite way leading to the same things, exhorting in these words: "Man was generated and constituted for the purpose of contemplating the reason of the whole of nature, and of wisdom: wherefore it is his duty to acquire and survey the intelligence of the things which truly exist." The "composite" referred to is this: with the peculiar nature of man he mingled the common because these can act in harmony with each other. For if the theoretic reason of man is conversant with the reason of the whole of nature, and the wisdom of man grasps and speculates upon the intelligence of the things which truly are, this being acknowledged, it is at once demonstrated that this [reason] is a part of universal reason and of the intellectual nature of the universe, and at the same time the exhortation becomes more perfect. For we do not live otherwise than in accordance with nature, which we all vehemently desire, unless we live in accordance with both human and divine reason; nor will we become happy unless by the aid of philosophy we acquire and contemplate the wisdom of truly existing beings.

Moreover, another "composite" element in this exhortation may be noted: it simultaneously incites to both theoretical and practical philosophy. For the acquiring of wisdom is the work or function of an effective and practical kind of philosophy, whose end is not the mere consideration of a thing but the apprehension of it by means of its activities. Contemplating, indeed, is the peculiar function of the theoretic intellect. To each of these, therefore, the exhortation pertains, and rightly. But since the good of wisdom becomes more apparent when it becomes more common and extended to all things, so also a more perfect exhortation to it arises, which Archytas expresses thus:

> Wisdom is not conversant with a certain particular one of the things which are, but is absolutely conversant with all the things which truly exist. And it is requisite that it should not first investigate the principles of itself, but the common principles of all beings. For the relation of wisdom to all beings is the same as that of sight to all things visible; and it is the function of it to know and contemplate the universal qualities of all things. And on this account wisdom discovers the principles of all beings.

Here again he does not confine or limit the energy of wisdom to a certain part [or separate thing] but says that it extends in common to all beings, and that it investigates the principles of all things and contemplates these in their genera by the most simple intuitions, in the same manner as the sight seizes the things seen.

Moreover, he adds that it comprehends universally the reasons or productive principles of all things, and with reference to this end it speculates and reasons discursively. Hence that science alone is not based on an hypothesis, because it discovers the principles of all beings and is able to give the reasons for its own characteristic principles. Rightly, therefore, was this mode of exhortation constituted. For if we are unable to apprehend by a reasoning process of such a wisdom either what is more universal, or perfect, or common, or self-sufficient, or good, or beautiful, certainly this apprehension should be sought by those who wish to acquire felicity through reason and intellect.

Lastly, the exhortation ascends to that which is highest as follows:

> Whoever is able to reduce all the genera under one and the same principle, and again to gather up and reckon them together, appears to me to be the wisest of men and to possess the most perfect veracity. He will also have discovered a beautiful place of survey from which he will be able to behold divinity and all things which are in coordination with and successive to him, subsisting separately or distinct from each other. Having likewise entered this most ample road, being impelled in a right direction by intellect, and having arrived at the end of his course, he will have conjoined beginnings with ends, and will know that God is the beginning, middle and end of all things which are accomplished according to justice and right reason.

Here he posits the end or purpose of the theological exhortation quite clearly. He considers that it does not involve numerous principles and all the genera of being; rather, he argues vigorously that all the genera which are contained under one and the same principle should be analyzed, and those enumerated natures which are nearest to the one principle should be separated from it. Thus continuing to contemplate ever more distant and separated natures, with the composite formed of the many and the one he composes and reckons together the multitude of things according to the reason-principle (*logos*) of numbers. Proceeding in this fashion to each part, he at one time recalls himself from the multitude to the one and at another descends from the one to the multitude.

But since we specially desire truth and wisdom, the exhortation leads to such a knowledge of the one all those who are truly versed in the theoretic science, and this is the end or summit of all contemplation. And he introduces the good, which is even more excellent than this, from which as from a watch tower we are able to behold Divinity and all things which are in coordination with it. For if Divinity is the author and basis of all truth, felicity, essence, cause, and principle, we should certainly work ardently to acquire that science by which one will be able to behold the Deity pure, and through which he will find the broad or true road leading to him, and through which he will conjoin ends with beginnings. For of such a kind is the most perfect life and felicity, which perceives by no longer separating the ends from the first beginnings, but collecting each of these into one containing simultaneously the beginnings, middle and end. For such is the nature of the divine cause, which it is necessary for those to adhere to who desire to reach the state of felicity. Thus, therefore, the exhortation considers all the things which are in us and in nature, and, so to speak, through all beings, and finally sums up or reduces all the modes of exhortation into one, namely that which leads to the Divinity.

V. It is right that from now on we should use the Pythagorean divisions of exhortation. For the disciples of this school followed the teachings of their master most skillfully and perfectly. They divided the mode or discussion by which they incited to the study of Philosophy differently from other schools, ingeniously strengthening and confirming it by most scientific demonstrations, deducing nothing but what follows logically from the premises. These divisions are as follows: All men desire to be happy, but we are happy if we possess many goods. Of goods some are of the body, in order that it may be naturally equipped with symmetry, due proportion, and strength; others are in external things, as, for instance, noble birth, power, and political honors in one's native land; others are of a psychical character, such as chastity, justice, courage—and, above all, wisdom or insight. In connection with these goods it is important that we secure felicity by right actions, and this felicity either comes from wisdom or arises by reason of its own inherent power. But we will not suddenly become happy by the mere possession of goods unless they benefit us in some way. But they will not in any way benefit us, even if they are present, unless we use them. For nothing benefits another merely by its presence, unless it is used by its possessor; nor if one is rich, and possesses what we are now referring to as "goods," but does not use them, will he be happy merely on account of their possession.

And so it is necessary that he who wishes to acquire felicity should not only possess such goods but also use them, because possession alone is of no value. Moreover, use alone does not suffice, but it is necessary to use them *rightly*. It matters much, indeed, whether one uses anything wrongly, or if he entirely neglects it: for the one is an evil, but the other is neither an evil nor a good. In the use of goods also, and in everything to be done, science will suggest or discover the right use. And as to the use of the goods of which we first spoke—namely riches, health and beauty—it is science which teaches the right use of these and shows the right way to act. Wherefore science supplies not only felicity but the right reason of action to men in everything which they possess and do, nor will other possessions or property be of any advantage to them without prudence and wisdom. For what advantage is it to possess many things and do many things, rather than a few, if one lacks intellect? Indeed, does not he who does a few things wrongly sin less than he who does many, and is not he who sins less a doer of less evil? And doing less evil will he not be less miserable? These things must be conceded, and equally the fact that he who possesses the goods mentioned without intellect will do more evil, and the one lacking them will do less.

Therefore, in summary, all the goods which we first noted are not in the opinion of the Pythagoreans goods *per se* or of themselves— and, indeed, such is the fact. If ignorance inspires and dictates the use of them they will become greater evils than their contraries, because they have more power to serve an evil leader: but prudence and wisdom, the greater goods, are not *per se* of value to anyone [but he must know how to use them]. Therefore Wisdom alone is good, and ignorance alone is evil. Since, therefore, we all strongly desire to be happy, it is plain that we will become so by using things, and rightly using them, but science brings to us rectitude and felicity: it would seem therefore that every man would endeavor in every possible way to become most wise, since this alone of all things—namely wisdom or insight—makes a man happy and truly prosperous. It is essential, therefore, that those wishing to become happy should philosophize [love and acquire knowledge].

But philosophy is the desire for and the possession of science, not the desire which is only skilled in getting apparent goods, or that which is only productive of them and does not use them. It is necessary that science be of such a character that in it the producing, the product, and the use of the product concur. If therefore all the sciences seek for and are preparative or procurative of goods, but perfect justice and insight alone show the equitable use of everything, and subordinate this use to intellect alone as the leader, then it is evident that it will be necessary to acquire insight and justice. For wisdom or insight contains in itself the contemplative and judicial power, and also the principles of the right use of goods, through whose acquisition we will pass through the remaining part of life nobly and felicitously.

Such is the exhortative way assumed from this first division. But there is another similar division among them. One thing in us is the soul, but another is the body: the soul rules and the body is ruled; and the soul uses, but the body is of such a nature that it is used. The soul is divine and good and most peculiar to and characteristic of us; the body is otherwise, being attached to the soul in the capacity of a servant or instrument, and being of advantage or use to the common life of man. Wherefore we should by all means care more for and attentively cultivate the ruling principle and not that which is ruled—our more divine and characteristic nature, and not that which is inferior or subordinate. Similar to this is that division by which all that pertains to us is divided in a triadic manner into soul, body, and the possessions of the body. Of these some are primary, others secondary, and other tertiary. Before all one should cultivate the powers of the soul, for other things are done for the sake of the soul. For the body should be cared for in such a way

that the attention given to it may contribute to the service of the
soul. It is necessary to acquire material goods through the body, but
to arrange all things for the sake of the soul and the ruling powers
of the soul. But if this be true, they do nothing of what is right who
concentrate all their energies on the acquisition of wealth but
neglect justice, through which we may learn how to use wealth
rightly; carefully attend to the life and health of the body, but
neglect to use rightly such life and health; and finally, cultivate
another form of discipline through which they cannot in any respect
secure a harmonious relation of the conflicting elements of human
nature, but ignore the science which is especially productive of
harmony or unity, which comes best through philosophy alone.
They attempt to do things, but in what way any particular thing
should be done, they neither know nor care.

From another standpoint they divide as follows: doubtless each
individual, his possessions, and what pertains to him are different.
Each of us is a soul, but that which belongs to the soul is the body,
and the possessions of the body are goods obtained for the sake of
the body. There are therefore three sciences in relation to these
three things. He who knows only the possessions of the body knows
what is his, but does not know himself. Hence the physicians do not
know themselves as such or so far as they are physicians, nor do the
gymnastic trainers; and those are still more remote from self-
knowledge who know the things about the body by which the body
is cared for, such as husbandmen and other manual laborers; these
are far indeed from knowing themselves. In fact, they do not even
know their own possessions. Wherefore those arts are rightly
deemed mechanical or illiberal. Temperance [self-control] alone is
knowledge of the soul, and in truth our virtue is that alone which
makes the soul better. It is right therefore that those should
specially strive to acquire this, who wish to regulate their life
conformably to their essence, and make themselves beautiful and
good, and intend to truly care for themselves.

To the same effect this may be added: Of all our possessions, after
the Gods, one's soul is the most divine and characteristic and
intimate. But a man's possessions are in every respect twofold: the
one superior and better, which governs; and the other inferior and

worse, which serves. And the things which govern must be preferred to those which serve. Thus, therefore, the soul, after the
Gods, must be honored before all other things. He does not honor
the soul who makes her worse than she was before, nor he who fills
her full of evils and remorse, nor he who refuses to endure praise-
worthy labors, and fears and sorrows, and pains, for by such
conduct he dishonors her; nor he who flees from "death," for such a
one is unable to endure the separation from the body and the life of
the soul *per se* or of and for itself; nor he who honors before virtue
beauty or wealth, for he thereby makes the soul which is better
inferior to those things which are worse. Therefore the one honor
of the soul will be a life according to right reason, and a perfection
of the soul according to intellect, and the becoming similar to the
best exemplars, and in rendering such things as are worse the
better so far as they are able to become better, and the flying from
evil—and, in addition, the hunting for and choice of that which is
the best of all, and then to constantly associate with it during the
rest of life. But this is nothing else than to philosophize rightly, so
that from every point of view those that desire felicity must
philosophize.

The following division brings us entirely to the same conclusion.
There are three forms of the soul: the first by which we reason [the
rational], the second by which we are courageous [the spirited], and
the third by which we desire [the desiderative]. Each of these has
characteristic motions of its own. Any one of these parts or elements, therefore, which is indolent and keeps its motions inactive
becomes most feeble, but it becomes very strong by the exercise of
its powers. Wherefore we should be careful that the motions of the
respective elements are harmonious with each other. And especially the principal part of the soul, which God has given to
everyone as a dæmon, and which elevates us from the earth to our
celestial affinity [cognate place]. Moreover, since we have not a
terrestrial but a celestial nature, this element must be specially
and chiefly cultivated and exercised. Now he who vehemently
labors to satisfy the cravings of desire and ambition will have none
but mortal thoughts, and will himself become mortal so far as it is
possible; and he is most absent from this celestial condition when

he fosters the mortal nature. But he who is strenuously devoted to the acquisition of knowledge and true wisdom, and employs his most vigorous exertions in this one pursuit—this man, if he grasps the truth, must necessarily have thoughts which are immortal and divine, and so far as it lies in human nature to possess immortality, he lacks nothing thereof; and since he ever cherishes the divine, and keeps in good estate the guardian spirit which dwells within him, he must be happy above all. And the care of this for every man is the same, namely, that he give to each part its appropriate motions and nourishment.

Now to the divine part of us are akin the motions, thoughts and revolutions of the whole [universe]. These every man should follow, restoring the revolutions in our highest part that are corrupted by our wanderings about generation, by learning the harmonies and revolutions of the universe so as to render the thinking soul like the object of its thought according to her primal nature: and when he has made it similar, he will obtain the end of that most excellent life which was set by the Gods before mankind for time present and time to come. For indeed it is not profitable to make the multifarious monster, Desire, strong by feeding him, nor is it right to nourish the lion, the spirited [courageous] element, and its members, and make them strong in us, while starving and weakening the man, the rational element, to such an extent as to leave him at the mercy of the guidance of either of the other two, without making any attempt to habituate or reconcile them to one another.[7] Much more, indeed, must the divine man in us be made the master of the many-headed beast, nursing and rearing the tame parts of it, and checking the growth of the wild, making the nature of the spirited element [the lion] his ally; and thus to pursue his training on the principle of concerning himself for all jointly, and reconciling them to one another and to himself. And he who so acts will be best in every respect, while he who acts otherwise has nothing of sanity. And in the superior character integrity [beauty and honesty] shines forth, for by the divine element the brutal [irrational] part of our nature is subjugated.

7) Cf. Plato, *Republic*, 589.

It is disgraceful for a man to be in a contrary condition: for then the gentle is enslaved by the wild, and the best by the most wicked, and the divinest part of himself is enslaved by the most ungodly and accursed, which does great injustice and injury to his soul. And, indeed, intemperance has been censured time and again for the reason that, during its outbreaks, the appetitive or desiderative element receives more liberty than it ought to have; again, arrogance and discontent are censured when the spiritual element grows and increases out of all harmony or beyond the right proportion; again, luxury is censured because it effeminates man by begetting cowardice in him; and finally, the names of flattery and servility are rightly used whenever one subjugates the spirited element to the turbulent monster, while to gratify this animal's insatiable craving for money he trains the spiritual element from the first, by a long course of insult, to become an ape instead of a lion. Moreover, other evils flow from this fount which debauch the best element of our nature. Therefore only by being governed by our divine and prudent element will we be happy.

Thus, so far as nature permits, all will be alike and friends, subject to the same government. This is plainly the intention of law, which is the common friend of all the members of a state, and also of the government of children, which consists in withholding their freedom until the time when we have formed a constitution in them, as we would in a city, and until, by cultivating the noblest principle of their nature, we have established in their hearts a guardian and a sovereign, the very counterpart of our own—then we allow them to be free. Therefore, the man who has intellect will direct all his energies through life to this one object: in the first place honoring those studies which will impress the highest character upon his soul, while at the same time despising all others. And as for his bodily habit and support, in the second place—far from living devoted to the indulgence of brute, irrational pleasure, he will show that even health is not primarily an object with him, and that he does not attach preeminent importance to the acquisition of health or strength or beauty, unless they are likely to make him temperate; because, in keeping the harmony of the body in tune, his constant aim is to preserve the symphony which resides in the soul, which must be done if one wishes to become a true musician [philosopher].

In the acquisition of wealth, too, he will avoid increasing it to an indefinite extent, which would bring him endless troubles and cares, but will look to his inward constitution or polity and be very careful lest any of his elements therein should give way owing to a superabundance or scantiness of substance. Holding by this principle he will to the best of his ability add to or spend his pecuniary means. And, finally, in reference to honors—with the same standard constantly before his eyes—he will be glad to taste and partake of those which he thinks will make him a better man; but he will shun, in private and in public, those which he thinks likely to break up his existing condition or habit of rectitude. And it is plain that, wasting no time on other things, he will concentrate all his energies on one thing, namely the acquisition of wisdom [insight], and will do all things subject to the guidance and supremacy of intellect. This is nothing else than to philosophize: so that, according to this division, above all it is specially necessary that those should philosophize who wish to become happy.

To the same end the following way also leads. All nature, which is as it were gifted with reason, does nothing in vain, but does all things for the sake of some end—and, banishing the aimless, is more intent on doing all things on account of some purpose than the arts, because the arts are imitations of Nature. Man is by nature a composite of soul and body, the soul being better than the body; and the better by virtue of its intrinsic superiority always rules the worse, and the body exists for the sake of the soul. One element of the soul is rational, but another irrational, which last is the inferior; so that the irrational element exists on account of the rational, and the rational for the sake of intellect: wherefore the demonstration forces the conclusion that all things exist for the sake of the intellect. Again, the thoughts of intellect are activities, being the perceptions by which we see or apprehend intelligibles, in the same manner as it is the function of the eyes to see things which are visible.

So for the sake of thought and intellect all things are desired and sought by men: if some are sought on account of the soul, but

intellect alone is the best of the psychical powers, for the sake of the
best the other things subsist. Also, of thoughts some are rightly
named free, because they are chosen for their own sake alone;
others are similar to slaves in that they are acquired for something
other than their own intrinsic value, namely action or work. Better
everywhere is that which is sought for itself alone than that which
is desired on account of another, because that which is free is
superior to that which is not free. Since actions therefore are used
by thoughts, thought perceives the utility of actions and so rules
them; nevertheless it follows these [in dealing with the material
world] and needs the service of the body: by means of these it is also
filled with fortune—for the sake of which it causes actions, of which
intellect is the master—and many things are done by the aid of the
body. Of thoughts, therefore, those which are sought on account of
pure contemplation are more honorable and better than those
which are desired for their utility in relation to other things.

Through and of themselves contemplations are of inestimable
worth, and in these the wisdom of intellect must be sought: but if
actions are assigned the thoughts which pertain to prudence,
practical judgment must be acquired. Hence the good which is
strong by reason of its own excellence and is inherent in the
contemplations of wisdom will in no respect be found in vulgar or
other contemplations. For plainly every notion is not of worth and
value but only that which comes from the Supreme Wisdom and is
in harmony with the government of the universe, for this is cognate
to wisdom and rightly subject to it. Man deprived of sense and
intellect together is reduced to the condition of a plant; deprived of
intellect alone he becomes a brute; deprived of irrationality but yet
remaining in the possession of intellect he becomes similar to God.
We must, therefore, exterminate to the extent of our power the
passions or affections of the irrational element, but use the pure
energies or functions of intellect with reference to itself and the
divine, and practice diligently to live in accordance with the
intuitive ways of intellect, using and applying to the attainment of
this end the whole attention of our intellectual eye and of love.

For we must not contemplate the Deity and divine things for the
sake of actions. For it is not lawful, they say, to defile the vision of

the divine by enslaving it to the necessity of that which is useful to men; nor is it right in any respect that the intellect should be drawn down to the consideration of these necessities: for the intellect alone of all the powers which we have is superior to fortune. Again, actions and all other things must be viewed and regulated with reference to intellect and Deity, and in accordance with this principle and what is right in particulars the irrational must be judged. For justice and judgment according to worth are alone able to procure true felicity for men. Note that the nature by which we surpass other animals alone shines forth in the contemplative or theoretic life, in which there is nothing fortuitous or anything of little worth. Of reason and prudence, indeed, other animals have some slight glimpses, but of theoretic wisdom which dwells with the Gods alone, they are entirely destitute. However, in the accuracy of the senses and the vigor of instinctive powers man is surpassed by many animals—but that alone is truly good which cannot be taken away and which contains the pure idea of good, since the upright man during his life in nowise or respect subjects himself to fortuitous things, but, on the contrary, from all those things controlled by fortune specially liberates himself. Wherefore even in this life of chance and trouble it is evident that we always and under all circumstances may be of good courage. For of what beatitude can he be deprived, who long ago estranged himself from those things which may be taken away, and who possesses his true self, lives within and of himself, and is nourished by himself and the infinite, by which he is united to Deity? Let these therefore be the Pythagorean exhortations to the study and acquisition of the most perfect wisdom.

VI. But since we are speaking to men and not to those having naturally the divine allotment of life [i.e. the Gods], it is right that we should mingle with these exhortations admonitions relating to the civil and practical life. These, therefore, follow. Those things which are subject to us in our life, as the body and those things about or connected with the body, were given to us as certain instruments. Of these the use is dangerous, causing much injury, for those who do not use them rightly. It is necessary, therefore, to seek and acquire scientific knowledge, and to use it rightly, by means of which we may use all these instruments properly and without detriment. We must philosophize, accordingly, if we wish to become a good citizen and to pass through life usefully. Moreover, there are some sciences which procure the things which are of gain or practical advantage in life; others which teach how these advantages are to be used; others which minister to our wants; others which rule, and in these the more primary sciences may be perceived which reveal that which is truly good. If that science which alone has the power of rightly judging, and using reason and contemplating the universal good, which is philosophy, is able to use all things and rule them according to nature, we certainly should philosophize in every possible way, because philosophy contains in herself right judgment and insight which is unerring and imperative.

In addition, since we all choose the things which are possible and useful, it is demonstrated that in philosophizing each of these subsists, and that the toil necessary to possess the philosophic power is less than the magnitude of its utility. For we all labor more pleasantly in things of easy acquisition. And that this is the case with things which are just and useful, and likewise with nature, and with the knowledge of any truth which we are able to apprehend, it is easy to demonstrate. For things primary are always more clear than the secondary, and the better nature more clear than the worse. For of what is definite and determinate there is more knowledge than of contraries, more of causes than of effects. Goods are more definite and ordered than evils, as an upright man is more controlled than one who is depraved—since it is necessary, by the same reasoning, that these differ from each other: much more do the primary causes differ from the secondary. For if the prior causes are destroyed, those things are destroyed which have their subsistence from them: magnitudes are destroyed if numbers are removed; superficies if magnitudes are removed; solids if planes are removed; elements if solids are removed.

Wherefore, if the soul is better than the body, for it is by nature more fitted to rule, and there are certain arts and exercises connected with the body, such as the medical and gymnastic—which we consider as sciences, and affirm that some possess them—then it is evident that there is equally about the soul and psychical powers a certain care and art which we are able to master, since we can know more difficult things of which there is greater ignorance. The same may be said concerning the things of nature. For it is necessary that there should be a much greater knowledge of causes and elements than of effects. For effects are not of the highest order of being nor do primary natures come from them, but from them and by means of them other things evidently arise and are constituted. For if fire, or air, or number, or some other natures are the causes and principles of other things, it is impossible for those who are ignorant of these to acquire knowledge of other things. For how could anyone understand a discourse who was ignorant of syllables, or know the syllables who knew nothing of their components?

Because, therefore, of truth and the psychical virtue or power there is a science or philosophic knowledge, and we are able to apprehend it, let these remarks suffice upon this point. But that philosophic knowledge is the greatest and most useful of all goods is evident from these facts. For all acknowledge that the most worthy and best by nature should rule, and that law alone should be the basis of government and the supreme principle. But law is a kind of wisdom and standard proceeding from the higher wisdom. Is there for us a better rule or canon, or a more accurate standard of good, than a truly wise man? Whatever, then, the philosopher seeks and acquires, guided by science, will be good, and the contrary of these will be evil. But since all specially choose those things which are in harmony with their natural dispositions and character—for the just man chooses a just life, the courageous a courageous, the modest a modest—so, likewise, it is plain that the wise man will choose wisdom or insight above all other things, for this is the characteristic function of insight. It is evident, therefore, that according to the highest or best judgment wisdom is the most excellent of goods. Therefore philosophy must not be shunned, if philosophy is, as we think, the possession and use of wisdom, and wisdom is the greatest of goods. Nor is it right or sensible that one should, for the sake of wealth, sail to the pillars of Hercules, and often incur dangers, but on account of wisdom should neither toil nor spend anything of either time or money. Indeed it is a servile or brutal manner of living, but not of living well, for one to eagerly desire and follow the opinions of the multitude of mankind, but to be altogether unwilling to imitate the industry and toil of the same multitude by seeking real wealth, the things which are truly beautiful. And thus the importance and utility of the pursuit of wisdom are sufficiently demonstrated.

That philosophy is much easier to acquire than other goods may also be shown. For though no reward is offered by men to those who devote themselves to the study of philosophy, by means of which they could have been encouraged to begin and continue this study, with the result that it is necessary that they should devote much time to other arts and work, nevertheless in a comparatively short time they attain accuracy in philosophic reasoning. This is evidence that the power of philosophizing may be easily acquired. Moreover, the fact that all gladly apply themselves to this study and wish to be conversant with it, ignoring all other things, is no small argument that this study is attended with constant pleasure. For no one wishes to toil a long time [without result]. In addition to this, the use of philosophy differs in the greatest degree from all other things. For its work neither instruments nor places are needed; but even as in any place whatsoever one may use his discursive reason (*dianoia*), so also he may everywhere grasp the truth which is always before him. It is therefore demonstrated that Philosophy is able to apprehend the highest of goods, and is the highest good, and that it is easy to acquire the possession of it. In sum, by reason of all the premises, it is fully worthy of the most zealous efforts to acquire it.

VII. One may see the same even more clearly from this consideration: wisdom and knowledge are desired by men *per se,* or for and of themselves. For without these they are unable to live as men or rational beings. And these are also useful to life, for no good comes to us unless it is caused by rational processes and wise actions. And, indeed, the felicity of life, whether it consists in pleasure[8] or in the possession of virtue,[9] or in wisdom, must be procured by means of

8) A reference to the Epicureans.
9) A reference to the Stoics.

philosophy. For these absolutely and above all come to us through philosophizing. Moreover, one part of us is soul and another is body: one rules, and the other is ruled; the one uses, and the other is used as an instrument. And always to that which rules and uses is related that which is ruled and used as an instrument.

Of the soul one element is reason, which by virtue of its nature rules and judges about our affairs; another, the irrational element, naturally obeys and is ruled by it. For everything that is well disposed according to its peculiar or characteristic virtue to have reached this condition—i.e. the condition where the characteristic power governs—is good. And when those natures which are highest and most primary and excellent have attained virtue, then they are well disposed.

That is better which is by nature more adapted to rule and to be principal, which is the relation of man to other animals. The soul therefore is better than the body, since it is constituted to rule; and in the soul are reason and discursive reason (*dianoia*). For the soul is of such a nature that it urges and checks, and says what to and what not to do. Of this part, therefore, the virtue, whatever it may be, is that which must necessarily be desired and chosen by us, and by all as specially and absolutely the best of all things. For we are safe in saying that it is by virtue of this element [reason] that we are entitled to be called men. Because when anything performs its natural work or function, not according to accident or by an alien strength, but in the best manner by its own inherent power, then it must be said that this is good and that this virtue is the principal or standard according to which each thing does that which it is naturally adapted to do. And of that which is composite and divisible, there are many and different modes of action; but of that which is simple and has a nature not dependent on another, it is necessary that there be one virtue which is peculiarly characteristic of itself. If, therefore, man is essentially a simple animal, and his essence is constituted of reason and intellect, his peculiar work or function is no other than a most accurate knowledge of truth and a true judgment about beings. But if he is a composite of many powers, it is plain that if an entity is naturally able to do many things the best of these is always its characteristic work, as, for example, the best product of the art of the physician is good health, and of a ruler the welfare of the citizens. But there is no better work of the soul or of that element of the soul which reasons discursively than the acquisition of truth.

The acquisition of truth, therefore, is the most principal or primary function of this element of the soul. This part acts simply according to science, and specially according to the science indicated by this name: but the chief end to this is contemplation. For when of two things one is chosen on account of the other, that one is the better and more eligible for the sake of which the other is chosen, as, for example, pleasure is more desirable than pleasant things, health than healthy things, for these are said to be causal of those. Wherefore there is nothing more desirable than intellectual insight, which we affirm to be the power or function of our most excellent and superior element, if habit is compared with habit. For the element whose nature it is to know, and which is both separate and composite, is better than the whole soul, and the science of this element is virtue. Of this science none of the several virtues is the function, for it is superior to all; nor is the universal virtue of the soul, since the end which is effected is better than the science causing it; nor is felicity. For if it is causative of one thing, another will be causative of other things as, for example, architecture is the cause of a house, though it is not a part of it. But intellectual insight is indeed a part of virtue and felicity: for we affirm that felicity either is from this or is this. So according to this reasoning it is impossible that science should be causative of anything. For the end is better than that which is produced, but nothing is better than wisdom or intellectual insight unless it is one of those which have been noted—but of these none is the work of it. Therefore it must be said that this science is theoretic alone, because it is impossible that its end can be an effect. Wisdom and contemplation, therefore, are the work of Virtue, and this is to be sought by men above all other things in the same manner as one seeks the power of seeing with the eyes, which one desires to have even if nothing else than the seeing itself comes to him on account of this power. Indeed, if we love the power of seeing *per se,* this fact alone sufficiently testifies that we all especially desire to become wise and know.

Moreover, if one loves anything which comes to him by means of something which is different from himself, it is plain that he will more desire whatever possesses this to a greater degree. For example, if one desires to walk because it is healthy, but running is still more healthy, and he knows and is able to do this, he will the more desire to do this by reason of his knowledge. If therefore true opinion is similar to wisdom, and if true opinion is only so far desirable as it is similar to wisdom on account of truth, and if this truth subsists more in wisdom, then wisdom must be desired and sought more than true opinion.

Now life is differentiated by the power of perception from that which is non-vital, and by the presence of perception and activity life is defined; and if the perceptive power is taken away, life becomes nothing, being as it were destroyed through the ablation of perception. Among the senses the power of perceiving or seeing is superior because it is most unerring, and it is on this account that we specially desire it. But every sense is a gnostic power by the aid of the body, just as, for instance, the sense of hearing apprehends sounds through the ears. Wherefore, if life is desired on account of sense, but sense is a certain species of knowledge; and if, moreover, because we are able to know things by means of sense we desire life, of two things that one is always more desired in which what is desired subsists to a greater degree, as we have shown before, then it is necessary that sight be the most excellent and most specially desired. But more than this and all the other senses and life itself is wisdom to be desired, because it is more receptive of truth, so that all [rational] men specially strive to acquire wisdom. For if they love life it is in order that they may gain insight and knowledge. For through no other reason do they value physical life than on account of sense-perception and especially the sense of sight: they appear to love this particular sense exceedingly because, compared with the other senses, it is as it were a species of direct cognition.

VIII. Our proposition is equally proven by common notions, i.e., by those things which are obvious to all. For it is evident to all that no one would desire or choose life, even if endowed with the greatest power and wealth of men, on the condition that he was to become estranged from Wisdom and insane—not even if he should enjoy the most intense corporeal pleasures in life, as some of the insane do. For this reason, as it appears, all specially flee from ignorance. But the contrary to ignorance is wisdom; and of things which are contrary to each other, one is to be fled from, and the other is to be sought. People similarly flee from disease and seek to be healthy. Wisdom or insight, therefore, it seems, according to this reasoning, must be sought above all things, nor is it one of the contingent things, as common conceptions testify. For if one should possess all other things but yet should be afflicted with a malady in that element of him which has wisdom, life would not be desirable, for all the other goods by and of themselves would be of no use to him. Hence all, so far as they apprehend Wisdom and are able to participate in it, think all other things to be nothing, and for this reason no one could endure to remain intoxicated or as a child during the whole of life. Likewise, sleep is indeed most pleasant, but is not to be desired perpetually, even if we allow all pleasures to the sleeper, because the visions or phantoms appearing in sleep are fallacious, but the perceptions of one who is awake are true. For sleep and wakefulness differ in no respect from each other except that while awake the soul often apprehends truth, and sleeping is always deceived. For the phantoms or images of ordinary dreams are altogether fallacious.

The fact that many flee from death shows the soul's love of knowledge. For the soul flies from what it does not know, the dark and the obscure, but naturally pursues that which is clear and knowable. And this is chiefly the reason why to those through whose physical instrumentality we see the sun and behold the light, our father and mother, we owe exceeding honor and reverence, as the authors of the greatest goods. But they are the causes to us, as it seems, of wisdom and sight. And through this same cause we delight in customs and things and men, and call those whom we know intimately and favorably our friends. These facts show plainly, therefore, that what is known, clear, and evident is lovable.

But if the known and perspicuous are lovable, it is evident that it necessarily follows that knowledge and wisdom are similarly lovable. It may be added that, as there is not the same reason for the acquisition of wealth as exists for the sake of living and living happily, so the same must be said about wisdom—there is not the same reason for merely living and for living well. And to the multitude there is much excuse, on account of ignorance, for doing this, i.e., identifying the two. For they desire felicity, indeed, but are content with a mere animal life. But whoever is not satisfied with merely living or vegetating will be ridiculous unless he undergoes every species of labor, and incurs trouble and vexation of every kind to acquire wisdom which enables him to know the truth. One may easily know this, if he will consider human life such as it really is. For he will find that those things which seem great and important to men are all mere shadows of reality. Whence it is rightly said that man [considered as an animal or creature of the senses] is nothing, and nothing of human things is permanent. For physical strength and magnitude and beauty are ridiculous and of no value; and beauty seems to be such only because we see nothing accurately or exactly as it is. For if one were able to see as keenly and piercingly as they say Lynceus was, who saw through walls and trees, how would he be able to bear the sight of anyone, seeing as he would of what evil materials a man is constituted? But honors, indeed, and glory, which they seek more than other things, are full of indescribable foolery. For to him who contemplates one of the eternal verities, it becomes absolutely silly to interest himself about these trifling things. For what of human things is enduring, or what is ancient?

But on account of our imbecility, I presume, and the brevity of life, this [physical existence] seems to be something great and important. Who therefore can think himself happy and blessed, beholding the evils in which we are involved by nature from the very first, by the way of punishment as it were, according to the interpreters of the Mysteries? For this indeed the ancients deem a divine saying, namely that the soul is now paying a penalty, and that our present life is a chastisement for heinous sins. Now the union of the soul and the body is precisely of this kind. Just as they say that the Tyrrhenians frequently torture their prisoners by binding dead bodies to living men so as to be in front of them face to face and limb to limb, so too the soul seems to be similarly stretched out and made fast to all the sensitive members of the body. Nothing therefore either divine or blessed subsists in man except the element of intellect and insight, which alone is worthy of any attention or study: for this alone of us is immortal and divine. And, moreover, the fact that we are able to participate in this intellectual power, though our life is naturally miserable and grievous, and yet is tempered with so much that is sensuously agreeable, demonstrates that in relation to other things on the earth man seems to be a God. For our intellect is a God, and our mortal life is a participant of a certain deity, as either Hermotimus or Anaxagoras said. Wherefore we must either philosophize—or, bidding farewell to physical life, go from this place, because all other things are full of trifles and rubbish. Thus one may apprehend from common conceptions the ways by which men are incited to apply themselves to the theoretic or contemplative philosophy, and specially to live the life of intellect, according to the teachings of true science.

IX. Beginning again, by considering the design or purpose of nature, we thus proceed to the same exhortation. Of those things which come into existence, some are generated by some type of discursive thought and art, such as a house or ship; for the cause of each of these is a certain art and thought, but other things come into existence through no art, but through nature. For of the generation of animals and plants nature is the cause, and all things of this kind come into existence according to nature. But some things come into existence through chance, neither through art, nor nature, nor necessity. Many of these, we say, come into existence through chance; and of the things generated by chance nothing comes into existence on account of anything, nor is there to them any end or purpose. But to those produced by art there is an end, and something for the sake of which they come into existence. For he who works by art will always give a reason to you explaining by what means and why he has designed anything, and this is better than that which comes into existence without an end or purpose. This is to be affirmed so far as art *per se* is alone the cause, unassisted by chance. For we properly consider the medical art to be more the cause of health than of disease; architecture the cause of the erection of a house, but not of its destruction. Everything therefore which arises through art comes into existence or is produced for the sake of something, and this is the best end of art. And that indeed which comes through chance, does not come into existence for the sake of anything: for though something good may come through chance, yet so far as it is according to chance and by chance it is not good, but always that which comes into existence from or according to chance is indeterminate or disorderly. But truly that which arises through nature is generated for the sake of something, and always on account of something better, as for instance is that which comes into existence through art. For nature does not imitate art, but art imitates nature; and it is the function of art to serve nature and fill up the gaps left by her.

For nature seems to be able to perfect some things *per se,* needing no aid; but other things scarcely, and others not at all, can she do *per se,* such as those which pertain to generation. Some seeds undoubtedly, wherever on the earth they may fall, will produce without care or attention, but others need the aid of the agricultural art. Similarly, some animals will develop spontaneously all their natural powers and instincts; but man needs for his preservation and protection many arts, both at the time of his birth and again in his development and growth. If therefore art imitates nature it will hence follow that whatever is effected through the arts comes into existence for the sake of something. For that which rightly comes into existence, we posit to be done for the sake of something; therefore that which is well generated is also rightly generated when it comes into existence. But all things which are produced according to nature are well produced, since that which comes into existence contrary to nature is worthless, and that which is produced according to nature is produced for the sake of something.

One may see this from an examination of each of our parts. For example, if you consider the nature of the eyelids you will see that they were not given to man for any purpose other than the protection of the eyes, that they might afford rest to them and prevent anything from falling upon them. Therefore the reason that something is produced and the reason that it ought to be produced are the same; as, for instance, if it is necessary make a ship in order that things may be carried on the sea—for the sake of this, it is made. And of the number of those things which are generated by nature, either all animals or the best of them are generated according to nature [i.e., perfect animals, not abortions or monstrosities, are generated according to nature]. For it matters nothing if anyone should think that many of them were generated contrary to nature, through some type of corruption and depravity. But man is the best and most worthy of all animals on the earth, so that it is evident that he was generated by nature and according to nature.

Pythagoras, being asked for what purpose or end Deity and nature created us, answered, "that we might contemplate the celestial sphere." And he said that he himself was a contemplator of nature, and in order to exercise this function came into physical life. And also Anaxagoras, being asked why anyone was born and desired to live, answered, "that he might contemplate the heavenly sphere and what it contains, the stars, moon, and sun, because all other things were nothing." So of everything the end or purpose is always better: for on account of the end all things that come into existence are generated, and that for the sake of which anything comes into existence is better and the best of all, and this is the end according to nature, and this end is that which, in the productive order fulfilling itself continuously, is the last to be perfected.

First, therefore, the things which pertain to the human body fulfill or attain the end, then those which pertain to the soul, and thus continuously the end or purpose of that which is better comes later than generation. Hence the soul is later in its entrance into the generated sphere than the body, and of psychical powers wisdom is perfected last. For we may see that this comes last to men in the order of nature, wherefore old age seeks this alone of the goods. Wisdom, therefore, according to nature, is to us an end, and the ultimate end or object for the sake of which we came into this world, i.e. that we may know. Therefore if we were generated, it is plain the purpose and object of our generation was that we may gain insight and learn something. Rightly for this reason did Pythagoras affirm that for the sake of knowing and contemplating was every man made by God. Whether the world or some other nature is to be contemplated may be considered later. This will suffice as a preliminary statement.

If Wisdom is the end according to nature, Wisdom will be the best of all things. Wherefore we should give attention to all other things on account of the goods which are in Wisdom, and of these goods we should bestow care on the corporeal for the sake of the psychical, but cultivate and practice virtue on account of Wisdom in which it resides, for this is the highest. But if one argues that from every science something else is produced, and that it is useful, he is totally ignorant of the primary difference between good and necessary things, and this difference is truly great. For those things which are loved on account of something else, things without which it is impossible to live, must be said to be necessary and concausal things. But the things that are loved *per se,* even though nothing else results from them, are properly called good. For one thing is not to be loved on account of another, and that on account of still another, for this process would continue *ad infinitum.* But it is necessary to stop somewhere. And it is utterly ridiculous, therefore, to require of every thing a utility besides the thing itself, and to ask of what benefit it is to us, and for what it is useful.

Truly may we say, if any one should as it were transport us in thought to the Islands of the Blessed—for there nothing "useful" is wanted, and nothing of all other things would be of any benefit, but alone would remain a life of thought and contemplation, that which we even now call a free life—in such a case who of us would not be justly ashamed if he were unable through his own fault to accept an offer of dwelling in the Islands of the Blessed? Wherefore the benefit of science to men must not be ignored: nor is it by any means a small good which arises from it. For just as we receive the rewards of justice in Hades, as the wise poets say, so do the gifts of Wisdom remain to us in the Islands of the Blessed. And so it is of no importance if Wisdom appears to be of no practical use to anyone. But we affirm that it is not useful but good; and that it should be chosen and sought, not on account of anything else, but *per se* or for its own sake alone. For just as we attend the Olympian festival for the mere pleasure of the spectacle alone, even though we gain nothing from it—for the spectacle is better than much wealth—and as we view the Dionysian performances, not that we may receive anything from the actors—truly we pay largely for the privilege of attending, and we spend much money in seeing many other shows, [which are not of a useful character]—so the contemplation of the universe must be preferred to all things which seem to be useful. Indeed it is not becoming that men should imitate weak women and slaves in contending and running with much ardor and trouble in order to see shows, and yet be unwilling to contemplate the nature and truth of beings without a utilitarian reward. Thus, proceeding from the purpose [design] of nature we have exhorted to the study and acquisition of Wisdom, as to a certain good which is valuable *per se* or for its own sake, even though nothing "useful" to human life should come from it.

X. But indeed that theoretic Wisdom or insight supplies to human life the greatest utilities, one may easily see from the arts. For just as learned physicians and gymnasts must be skilled in a knowledge of nature, so also good law-givers must have a knowledge of nature, and a much greater knowledge than the others. For the first are only artificers of corporeal virtue [strength], but the others are busied with the virtues of the soul, and the felicity and infelicity of the State—much more therefore do they need philosophy. For even as in other mechanical arts the best instruments are drawn from nature as, for instance, in carpentry the plummet, rule, and compass, the exemplars for which are found in water, light, and the splendors of rays by which we test those things which to the senses appear sufficiently straight and smooth, so likewise it is necessary that the politician should have certain standards drawn from nature and truth, in accordance with which he judges what is just, what is beautiful, and what is useful. For just as in nature the exemplars surpass all the instruments, so here that law is the best which approximates nearest to the natural or eternal law. This it is not possible for one to enact unless he philosophizes and knows the truth. And of other arts, they know that the instruments and most accurate reasonings are not assumed primarily from themselves but from things secondary, tertiary, and most remote, and the productive principles are drawn from experience.

To the philosopher alone is there a correct representation of those things which are of and from themselves accurate exemplars, immutable Ideas, for he is a spectator of things themselves but not of imitations of these. Just as neither will he be a good carpenter who does not use the rule and other instruments of this kind, but builds with reference to other houses as a rule or model, similarly, if one [without reference to immutable exemplars] establishes laws for states, or does things with reference to other actions, or imitates the human forms of states either of the Lacedæmonians or Cretans or others, he will be neither a good legislator nor an upright man. For it cannot happen that an imitation of that which is not good is good, nor that an imitation of that which is not divine and permanent may be immortal and permanent; but of all artificers and legislators the laws of the philosopher alone are permanent and the actions right and beautiful. For he alone who looks to nature and the divine truly lives, just as a good ruler drawing from immortal and stable sources the principles of living advances and lives according to them himself. This science therefore is both theoretic and productive, as we do all things according to it. For just as sight is neither productive nor causative of anything, since its sole function is to judge and make manifest everything visible, and to afford us the power and opportunity to act, so that by its aid the greatest deeds may be done by us—for deprived of sight we are practically helpless—so also it is plain that though true science is theoretic, we may by means of it do thousands of things, and through it may apprehend some things and avoid others; and briefly, may acquire all good through it.

XI. That to those who choose the life according to intellect comes also the most pleasant form of life, will appear from the following. It seems that word "life" or "living" has a twofold meaning: one which refers to the mere capacity to live, and the other to the activity of living. For we say that all animals see—both those which are endowed with sight and are thereby naturally able to see, even though they may close their eyes, and those who make an active use of the power of sight in relation to things. Similarly, there is a distinction between the words Science and Knowledge: the one signifying the theoretic faculty by which we apprehend real beings, the other the practical faculty by which we acquire phenomenal facts and information. If therefore by sense-perception living and non-living differ, the word 'sense-perception' is itself used in a twofold meaning: one signifying the active use of sense perception, and the other the mere capacity to use it. Hence also we affirm that he who sleeps has sense-perception. For it is plain that "living" has a twofold meaning. For he who is awake must be said to live truly and properly, and he who sleeps to live otherwise, because he has the capacity to pass into the state of activity, on account of which we say that he is "awake" and perceives things. Wherefore, and looking to this fact, whenever two entities are designated by the same word, but only one of the two is said to do or suffer something, to this one the descriptive name or predicate applies more than to the other—just as we affirm that he who uses science knows rather than he who merely possesses science; that he sees who directs his sight to objects rather than he who is merely able to see. For we not only say that the "more" or "greater" exists, when some particular individual among those things possessing one reason-principle surpasses the others, but also when one is prior and the other posterior. Thus we assert that good health is a greater good than health alone, and what is desirable *per se* by reason of its nature than that whose good or desirability is artificial or factitious, although in whatsoever way the name is applied we may perceive that each of the two is good, whether the discourse be about useful things or about virtue.

It must be said, therefore, that he who is awake lives more than he who sleeps, and he who actively uses the powers of his soul than he who only has them in capacity or potentially. For we affirm that the latter lives also on account of the former, because he is so constituted that he is able to do and experience the same things. Wherefore "use" or the useful is predicated of anything when, the capacity existing, some one brings it into activity; but if he deals with many things he will use the best of them as, for instance, if one uses flutes, he will play only or at least mostly with the best. Moreover, to this other things are similar. Therefore it must be said that he uses more or to a greater degree, who uses rightly. For he who uses anything rightly and accurately knows how to use it in the manner and for the purpose to which it is naturally adapted. But there is to the soul alone or above all other things the function of thinking and reasoning. It is a simple proposition, therefore, and easily to be deduced by anyone, that he lives more or gets the most out of life who thinks rightly and, above all, he who in the highest degree apprehends truth. This is he who wisely thinks and contemplates, according to the most accurate science.

And a perfect life must be conceded to those who are truly wise and intelligent. But if "living" is the same to every animal as its being or essence, it is plain that the wise man lives specially and principally; and particularly during the time when he acts and contemplates that which, of all things that truly are, is most knowable. And in a perfect and free activity itself there is a pleasure, so that theoretic activity or contemplation is the most pleasant or delightful of all. Again, it is one thing to drink without repugnance, and another to drink with pleasure. For nothing prevents one who is not thirsty from taking a drink which does not please him, and yet during the drinking he may be pleased, not by the act of drinking indeed, but by the pleasant sensation to his palate which accompanies it, just as external may be accompanied by internal contemplation.[10] We say, therefore, that to this one the drinking is agreeable and he is pleased, but not by the *act* of drinking, nor does he drink gladly. Thus also all walking and sitting and learning and every movement we affirm to be either pleasant or disagreeable; not that it happens that we in particular grieve or rejoice because such things are present, but by reason of their presence people generally grieve or rejoice. And similarly we affirm that life to be pleasant, whose presence is pleasant to those possessing it; and we declare that all do not live pleasantly to whom pleasure in life occasionally comes, but only those to whom life itself is pleasant, and who derive pleasure from life.

So we assert that the active lives more or to a greater degree than the dormant; the wise man more than the ignorant: further, we affirm that the pleasure derived from life, which arises from the right use of life, pertains to the soul, for this is to live truly. If

---

10) Kiessling says that he cannot fathom the meaning of this sentence. I have given what I conceive to be the sense of it, but the text is probably corrupt.

therefore the functions or powers of the soul are many, but the most excellent of all is that which essentially acquires insight, then it is evident that the pleasure which springs from wisdom and contemplation comes alone or principally from living theoretically: therefore a pleasant life and true pleasure come only or chiefly to philosophers. For the energy of the profoundest intellections drawn from true beings, and always steadily looking to the proposed perfection, is the most effective above all other things in producing genuine pleasure. Wherefore it is necessary that those who have intellect must philosophize, if they wish to acquire and enjoy true and pure pleasures.

XII. But if our conclusion is to be deduced not only from parts but from a consideration of universal felicity, we distinctly affirm that, in the same manner as philosophy is related to felicity, so is our moral perfection, having no connection with that which is vile. For all things, partly on account of Felicity and partly on account of Philosophy, are desired and sought by means of which we become happy. We therefore define Felicity to be either intellectual insight or some type of wisdom, or Virtue, or the greatest intellectual pleasure, or all of these. If therefore it is intellectual insight, it is evident that to philosophers alone will come a felicitous life; if it is psychical virtue, or intellectual pleasure, these also the philosophers either alone or above all others will experience. For Virtue is the most valuable and excellent of our possessions, and Wisdom is the most delightful of all things, comparing things with each other. Similarly, if one should say that all these constitute Felicity he would define Wisdom or Insight: wherefore all should philosophize to the extent of their capacity. For philosophy indeed is the science of living perfectly, and is above all things, to speak briefly, the cause to souls of this perfect life. Yet on this earth, because our race is in an unnatural abode, it is difficult for us to learn and investigate, and scarcely one is able on account of mental sluggishness, [caused by our descent hither], and the unnatural life, to acquire a perception of this fact. But if, saved, we return again to the place whence we came, it is evident that we will learn easily and pleasantly. For now, abandoning the pursuit of things which are truly good, we are devoting all our time to things which are termed 'necessary' or 'practical,' and this is especially the case with all those who seem to the multitude to be most happy. *But if we pursue the heavenly way and live in our kindred star, then we will philosophize, living truly, busied with the most profound and marvellous speculations, beholding the beauty in the soul immutably related to Truth, viewing the rule of the Gods with joy, gaining perpetual delight and additional insight from contemplating, and experiencing pure pleasure absolutely unmingled with any pain or sorrow.* Pursuing this way, therefore, we will find that Philosophy leads us to total felicity; and hence, since Philosophy is in its nature most excellent, it is fully worthy of our most ardent study.

XIII. But if it is necessary to use an exhortation to the study of Philosophy drawn from philosophic conceptions, we will thus begin. It seems that those who practice philosophy rightly are not understood by others to do nothing else than to study how "to die" and "to be dead."[11] And this very rationally. For the multitude do not know in what way and why true philosophers study how "to die," and are worthy of "death," and what kind of a "death" they deserve. And death indeed is nothing else than the release and separation of the soul from the body, and this is "to die": so that death is merely the existence of the body apart from the soul, and the existence of the soul *per se* or apart from the body. This therefore being so, it is not reasonable that the philosopher should eagerly pursue pleasures so-called—such as, for instance, the pleasures of eating and drinking, or sexual delights. Nor will he consider as of any worth the other services and cares of the body, such as the possession of costly clothing and sandals and other adornments of the body—these he will not deem of any importance but will despise them, and will use them only so far as it is absolutely necessary.

In brief, it seems that the study and business of this man is not concerned with the body, but, so far as he can, he departs from it, and applies himself absolutely to the culture of his soul. And in things of this kind it is plain that the philosopher, acting differently

11) Plato, *Phædo*, 64A-65D.

from other men, especially aims and studies to release his soul from an association with the body: and by reason of this fact the multitude thinks that to him who derives no pleasure from corporeal things, and who enjoys none of them, life is not worth living, but that he verges most closely on the state of death who cares nothing for the pleasures which come through and by means of the body. Moreover, in acquiring Wisdom the body is an impediment, if one should take it with him as a companion in the search. But to illustrate this point: neither the sense of sight nor of hearing brings any truth to men. For the poets constantly sing to us that "we nothing accurate hear or see." And if even these senses of the body are neither accurate nor certain, much less are the others: for all the others are inferior to these.

Wherefore, if the soul does not apprehend the truth when it attempts to investigate something in connection with the body— since it is evident that it is then deceived and misled by the body— it is doubtless in the process of thinking, if at all, that any real truth becomes manifest to her. But she thinks and reasons the best, most deeply and perfectly, when none of the senses annoys by its intrusion, neither hearing, nor sight, nor pain, nor any pleasure— and reaches after true being when she is as much as possible alone *per se,* bidding farewell to the body, and as far as possible, becoming free from communication and contact with it. Here, then, the soul of the philosopher most despises the body, and flies from it, and seeks to become and live alone *per se.* But this will be specially evident from the contemplation of Ideas. For absolute Justice, Beauty, and Good, and all other things on which we impress the character of essence or reality—no one ever saw any of these with his eyes nor perceived them by any other senses which act through the body; but whoever has most thoroughly and accurately prepared himself to apprehend intellectually the essence of each object of his investigation, he it is that will approximate the nearest to the knowledge of it. Wherefore he will do this most purely who strives to reach each thing as much as possible by discursive reason alone, and neither takes the sight as an accessory in the processes of the discursive power, nor drags after him any other sense to act in connection with his reasoning power; but using his discursive reason *per se,* in its absolute purity, he will strive to investigate and apprehend everything which is true being, subsisting pure and *per se,* liberated as far as possible from eyes and ears and, speaking summarily, from the whole body, because it only disturbs the soul and does not permit her by its presence to acquire truth and Wisdom. For this man, if any, will attain to true being.

From all the premises, therefore, it necessarily follows that such an inference will be drawn by genuine philosophers, that they will speak to each other thus: It seems that it is only a certain narrow way which will lead us to the end of our journey in this investigation, because so long as we have the body as an associate with reason in our search and our soul is mixed up with such an evil,[12] we shall never fully attain the object of our desires, and this object we affirm to be Truth. For innumerable are the impediments which the body throws in our way, on account of the necessity of providing for its support. Moreover, should any maladies befall it they too impede the ardent pursuit of real being—and it fills us with desires and passions and terrors and vain imaginations of all kinds and a host of frivolities, so that as it is truly said, *we can never truly and in reality acquire wisdom or insight through the body.* For in fact to wars, seditions, and contentions nothing else than the body and its passions incite us. For all wars arise through the passion for acquiring wealth, and we are compelled to get it on account of the body, because we are enslaved to its service; so that, on account of this, we have no leisure for the study and practice of philosophy.

But the last and worst of all is, that if any leisure from the exactions of the body should come to us, and we apply our mind to the speculation of any intellectual object, in the very midst of our researches again, at every moment, it interrupts us, creating tumult and disturbance, and confuses us so that we are unable, by reason of its presence, to perceive the truth: but in fact it has been demonstrated that, if we are ever to know anything purely and

12. Most Neoplatonists did not consider the body to be absolutely evil as Neoplatonism sees the natural world as a theophany, a manifestation of the divine. Iamblichus is more pessimistic in this regard as he thought that the soul descends entirely into the realm of generation, from which it must be released, while Plotinus, for instance, held that there exists a perfect, "unfallen" part of the soul, constantly contemplating the Forms in the realm of Nous or Mind.

clearly, *we must be liberated from the body, and contemplate with the soul alone the realities of things, i.e. the Ideas.* And then, as it appears, we shall have what we desire and profess a love for, namely Wisdom or insight, after "death," as our argument makes clear, but not so long as we "live."

For if it is impossible to attain to pure knowledge while we are associated and connected with the body, one of two things must follow: either we can nowhere at all acquire it, or only after death, for then, but not before, will the soul be by herself, separated from the body. And during our lifetime we shall, I think, make the nearest approach to knowledge, if we abstain as far as possible from intercourse and communication with the body, except so far as is absolutely necessary, and preserve ourselves from infection by its nature, keeping ourselves pure from its pollutions until God himself has liberated us from the corporeal bonds. And thus being pure, and released from the folly of the body, it is right to believe that we shall dwell with others who are similarly pure and genuine: for it is not lawful that the impure should ever associate with the pure. But purification, indeed, as has been said above, consists in the most complete separation of the soul from the body, and the habituation of her to collect and concentrate herself by herself from all parts of the physical frame, and to dwell as far as possible both in the time now present and in the future alone by herself, released from the body as from a prison, working out her deliverance as it were from the shackles of the body. But this is called "death," namely a release and separation of the soul from the body. But chiefly, and indeed only, those who philosophize rightly, as we have said, always work in the most strenuous degree to release the soul; and the aim and study of philosophers is neither more nor less than this, the release and separation of the soul from the body.

Wherefore philosophy, since it brings to us the greatest good, namely a liberation from the chains in which the soul is bound from the date of its birth into time must be sought with the most intense avidity and study. But what is called Fortitude chiefly belongs to those who are disposed to the study of Philosophy; and likewise Temperance, which even the many call by its right name, and which consists in not being agitated by the passions but in moder-

ating them with contempt and composure, belongs only to those
who specially despise the body and live in the practice of Philosophy. For if the Fortitude and Temperance of others are examined
they will appear to be absurdities. For it is well known that all
others deem "death" to be the greatest of evils. It is therefore from
fear of greater evils that the brave among the many support death,
when they do support it: therefore all except the philosophers are
courageous through and by fearing and fear, though it is strange
that one should be courageous through fear and timidity. But what
about the moderate among them? Are not these affected in the
same manner, being temperate through a kind of intemperance?
And yet, though we should be disposed to say that it is impossible,
still their case in respect of this foolish kind of temperance does
come to bear a close resemblance to this: for from mere fear of being
deprived of one kind of pleasures and from desire of another, they
abstain from some while they are dominated by others; and though
they call a subjection to pleasures intemperance, yet at the same
time they succeed in mastering some pleasures just because they
are mastered by others; and this is analogous to what was said just
now, that in a way they are made temperate through intemperance.
This, therefore, is not the right road to virtue, namely to change
pleasures for pleasures, pains for pains, fear for fear, and the
greater too for the less, like so many pieces of money; but Wisdom
alone is the coin for which we must exchange all these things, and
all that is bought and sold for this and with this—that and that
alone is in reality, whether it be fortitude or temperance or justice;
and in a word that true virtue only exists when accompanied by
wisdom, whether pleasures and fears and all the rest of such things
be thrown in or withdrawn: whereas, separated from wisdom and
exchanged one for the other, such virtue as this is a mere shadowy
sketch and really servile, with no soundness or genuineness about
it. But real Virtue is a complete purification from all such things;
and Temperance, Justice, Fortitude, and Wisdom itself form the
prelude as it were to this purification from pollution.

And indeed those famous men who established the Mysteries for
us seem to have been no mean thinkers, but in fact to have
obscurely hinted long ago that whoever descends into Hades

uninitiated and unpurified shall grovel in the mire; but he who has
been purified and initiated shall on his arrival there dwell with the
Gods. For there are, say those who write about the Mysteries, many
that bear the thyrsus [wand] but few that are bacchanals [true
initiates].

> The thyrsus-bearers numerous are seen,
> But few the Bacchuses have always been.[13]

These few are in my opinion no other than the genuine philosophers. If therefore philosophy alone by reason of its nature causes
perfect virtue and purification of the soul, that alone is worthy to
be desired and sought. But to the company of the Gods none may go
who has not sought wisdom and departed in perfect purity; none
but the lover of learning. And this is the reason why true philosophers abstain from the indulgence of all corporeal desires or
passions, and persevere in this abstinence, not surrendering themselves to them, and not at all because they fear ruin and poverty,
like the vulgar and the lovers of money: nor, again, because they
fear disgrace and contempt, like the lovers of power and of honor,
do they abstain from these desires. Wherefore those who have any
concern for their soul, and do not live subserving their bodies, bid
adieu to all such characters as we have mentioned, and walk not in
the same path, being assured that these know not where they are
going: but they themselves, persuaded that they ought not to act
contrary to philosophy and to its liberating and purifying opera-
tions, give themselves up to its direction, and follow whithersoever
it leads.

For the lovers of learning know that Philosophy receiving into its
care their soul which is a close prisoner in the body and glued to it
and forced to contemplate real things through the body, or as it
were through the bars of her dungeon, instead of alone, and
wallowing in every kind of ignorance, and clearly perceiving that
the dire nature of the dungeon arises through the soul's eager
desire or appetition to make as much as possible the captive himself

13) Plato, *Phædo*, 69C-D.

an accomplice in his own incarceration—the lovers of learning therefore know that Philosophy receiving their soul into its care in this condition gently endeavors to exhort her and to set her free, by showing her that all observation by the eyes is fallacious and illusive, and that this is likewise the case with perception, the ears and the other senses; and by persuading her to withdraw from them, except just so far as she must use them, and by exhorting her to collect and concentrate herself into herself, and to put no faith in anything but herself, that is, in that portion of real existence in and by itself which she can apprehend in and by herself, but whatsoever she contemplates by different organs varying with varying conditions—she holds none of that to be true, for all such things belong to the realm of sense and of the visible, *whereas what she sees herself belongs to the intelligible and invisible.*

Thinking, then, that she ought not to oppose herself to this process of liberation, the soul of the true philosopher therefore holds herself aloof from pleasures and passions and fears as far as possible, reflecting that, whenever anyone is violently moved by pleasure or fear or pain or desire, the evil that he contracts from them is not of that slight magnitude that one might think—an attack of sickness, for instance, or some loss incurred by the indulgence of his passions—but he suffers that which is the greatest and extremest of all evils, though he never takes it into account, namely that the soul of every man in the act of feeling some vehement pleasure or pain is at the same time forced into the belief that everything which most excites this feeling is the most vivid and true, though it is not so. And these are, most of all, the visible things.

Wherefore in this "feeling" the soul is most completely manacled by the body, because every pleasure and pain with a nail as it were fastens and rivets the soul to the body, causes her to become corporeal, and to believe that whatever the body asserts is true. For from her conformity of opinions and identity of pleasures with those of the body, she is forced to become like it in her habits and nurture, and of such a character that she can never arrive in Hades pure, but must always depart polluted by the body, so that she speedily falls again into another body, and grows again as if she had been sown there, and hence is deprived of all communion with that which is pure, simple and divine.

On account of these things [i.e., the considerations drawn from the nature and destinies of the soul] therefore the true lovers of wisdom are temperate and firm, and not for the reasons which the multitude assigns: but the soul of the philosopher reasons thus, and does not think that Philosophy ought to liberate her from the body, but that while Philosophy is freeing her she may give herself up to pleasures and pains so as to be again entangled in bonds, condemning herself to endless labor, handling, so to speak, her web in the very opposite way from the example of Penelope; on the contrary, calming the passions to rest, following her reason and in it ever abiding, contemplating that which is true, divine, and beyond the sphere of opinion, and being nourished by it, she deems that she must thus pass her life as long as it lasts, and that after "death" she will go to that which is akin and congenial to herself, and so be delivered from all human evils.

From this course of reasoning it is evident that Philosophy brings to us a release from human or corporeal chains and a deliverance from the incidents of temporal birth [generation], and leads to that which truly is, and to a knowledge of Truth itself and the purification of souls. But if in this above all things there is true felicity, we must cultivate philosophy most zealously, if we wish to be truly happy. Moreover, it is right to reflect that, since the soul is immortal, it requires our anxious care, not merely for this interval of time which we call "life," but always; and most serious will be the danger if we neglect the soul. For if death were a total annihilation, great would be the gain to the wicked, since they would be liberated by death at once from the body and from their depravity, together with the soul; but now, since the soul proves to be immortal, there is for her no escape from evils, nor salvation, other than by becoming as good and wise as possible.

For the soul descends to Hades with nothing whatever but her education and culture, which as it is said is [according to its kind] either of the greatest aid or of the greatest disadvantage to the soul, at the very outset of her journey thither. For the better soul dwells with the Gods, traverses the heavenly sphere, and receives a better allotment; but he who has been guilty of unjust acts and is full of depravity and impiety, going into the subterranean dungeons receives fitting penalties.

For the sake of these things, therefore, we ought to use our utmost efforts to gain virtue and wisdom in this life. For the contest is noble and the hope great, and on account of these one should believe confidently in the worth of his own soul if through life he has ignored corporeal and mundane pleasures as alien, and considered any participation of them as pernicious to himself, but has given himself to those pleasures which are inherent in learning—and, ornamenting his soul not with anything alien to its essence but with its own connate ornaments, namely wisdom, justice, fortitude, liberty, and truth, he is ready to take the journey into Hades when the appointed time arrives.

These things being so, we should not make the accumulation of riches our highest aim, nor glory and honor, but the acquisition of Wisdom and truth and the way by which the soul may reach the most excellent condition. Things of the greatest worth should not be held in less esteem than those of a trifling character. Neither, therefore, must attention be given to the body, nor to the getting of money, nor to anything else, prior to the care of the soul, which it should be our chief business to bring to the best possible condition. For Virtue does not arise from riches, but from Virtue come riches and all other goods, private and public, to men. This one thing, therefore, must be deemed absolutely true, namely that to a good man neither in life nor after death will any evil come, nor are his affairs neglected by the Gods; so that to him will be given all the goods which contribute to felicity, and he who closely follows the path leading to Virtue will live most happily. Let therefore an exhortation to the study of Philosophy, drawn from the preceding, be of this kind.

XIV. Next we must draw an exhortation from the life of philosophers of the first rank, the Coryphæans,[14] according to the teachings of Pythagoras. For these philosophers have never from their childhood known the way to the forum, or where a law court is, or

14) Plato, *Theatetus*, 173C-177B.

council chamber, or any other political meeting-place; laws and decrees, whether spoken or written, they neither hear nor see. The ambitious striving of political clubs for offices, public meetings, and banquets and revelings with minstrelsy—all these are practices which do not occur to them even in dreams. What has been well or badly transacted in the city, or what infamy may attach to anyone from his ancestors, either by his father's or mother's side, of this he is as ignorant as he is of the number of drops of water in the ocean. And he is even ignorant that he is ignorant of all these particulars, for he does not keep himself aloof from them for the sake of reputation; but in reality it is only his body which dwells and is conversant in the city, while his discursive reason (*dianoia*), deeming all these things trifling and of no value, despises them and soars all abroad, "measuring," as Pindar says, "the regions below the earth and those upon it, star-gazing into heaven's height," and thoroughly investigating all the nature of the beings which each whole contains, but not descending to anything which is near.

It is said, for example, that Thales astronomizing and looking intently upward fell into a well, and a bright and lively Thracian girl taunted him about the accident, saying that in his eagerness to know what was in heaven he could not see what was around him and under his feet. Now the same taunt is good for all students of Philosophy. They are indeed entirely ignorant what their nearest neighbor is about, and almost whether or not he is a human being; *but what man is, and what it becomes him, as distinguished from every other creature, to do or suffer, into all this they make diligent inquiry.*

Therefore when a philosopher of this kind chances to hold a public or private conversation with anyone, when he is compelled to enter a law-court, or some such place, and engage in a discussion concerning the things before his eyes and under his feet, he is a fruitful subject for merriment, not only to Thracian girls but to the whole company, tumbling into pitfalls and getting into all sorts of embarrassments because of his ignorance, and behaving so awkwardly that people look upon him as a kind of booby. If he is shamefully treated, he does not retaliate, as he has no private grudge, and he is regarded as ridiculously inspired because he knows no evil of anyone and is without any appetite for gossip. When others are praised and eulogized, he is only unfeignedly amused, and is for this also counted as a manifest simpleton. When he hears a tyrant or king praised, it is in his estimation much as if some herdsman, or swineherd, shepherd, or cow-herd, were praised for his large stock of serviceable beasts; with this difference, however, that he thinks of a herd of cattle as less treacherous and ungovernable than the animals tended and milked by a tyrant.

And as for the ruler, he must become even more rude and uncultured than a herdsman, for he is always hard at work and girt in by his stone walls as by the sides of a mountain cavern. When this philosopher hears that some one owns a thousand acres or more, this marvellous possession is for him an unconsidered trifle, since he has been wont to view the whole earth. They who sing of pedigree, how that some are noble because they count seven rich ancestors, are to him of dull and narrow sight, being unable in their ignorance to fix their eyes upon the whole of time or to reflect that everyone has had myriads of forefathers and ancestors, amongst whom are numbered rich and poor, kings and slaves, both barbarians and Greeks. When they boast that in their genealogical tree the five and twentieth ancestor was Hercules the son of Amphitryon, they forget in their petty arithmetic that Amphitryon's five and twentieth ancestor was nobody in particular, and that he in turn had a fiftieth; and the philosopher smiles at their meagre reckonings, and fatuous absorption in their own vain and foolish selves.

In all this, however, he is ridiculed by the multitude, in part because he has a proud bearing, as they think, in part because he is ignorant of what is at his feet, and in matters of detail is always at fault.

But when the philosopher leads anyone to take a higher view, and bids him mount out of questions of private injury into the consideration of justice and injustice, as each is in itself and as they differ from each other and from all other things, or when they turn from the question whether the rich king is happy to inquire into kingship and human happiness generally, of what nature they are and what kind of man ought to be happy and escape misery— when such questions as these are to the fore, and that narrow-minded legal personage must give a reason and answer, then he presents a counterpart of the philosopher. For, suspended aloft at such an unusual height and looking into mid-air, he becomes dizzy and dismayed, his want of wit and incoherent babble making him a laughing-stock, not to Thracian girls or any uneducated person, for they do not see the absurdity, *but to all whose training has not been that of slaves.* Such is the condition and character of each: one is that of the man really, bred in freedom and leisure, who should be given the name philosopher, who surely is not to blame if he is foolish and at a loss when it falls to him to perform some such servile duty as to pack a trunk, or flavor a sauce, or make a fawning speech; the other is the man who can do all these services thoroughly and with dispatch, but who does not know how to don his cloak gracefully, or, by acquiring harmony of language to sing well the true life of the Gods and blessed men.

I think, therefore, if all men were convinced of these things, there would be more peace and less evil in the world. But, indeed, evil cannot be altogether destroyed, for there must always be something opposite to good: it cannot, however, find a place in the home of the Gods, but of necessity flourishes in the mortal nature and this terrestrial region. Wherefore we must endeavor to fly from this world to the other with the utmost haste. Moreover, one should know that flight means becoming like to God as much as possible; and the way to be like God is to become just and holy and wise. But it is difficult to persuade the many that these are the true reasons for shunning evil and seeking Virtue, and not, as they think, in order to have the appearance of goodness. But the notions of the many on this subject are as absurd as an old woman's fable. The real truth may thus be stated: God can never be unjust, but is wholly just, and nothing can be more like Him than the perfectly just man.

By this means we distinguish genuine worth from worthlessness and puerility; for to know the nature of God is wisdom and true virtue, and not to know it is sheer ignorance and vice. All other wisdom [so called] or ability, whether in politics or in the arts, is vulgar and ignoble. It is far better not to allow for a moment that the men who are unjust, profane, or unrighteous in word or deed are men of powerful minds because they are rogues. Such men glory in their name, and imagine that they are spoken of not as good-for-nothing encumbrances but as exemplary citizens. They must be told that their worthlessness is in proportion to their false opinion of their value. They are ignorant of what they most of all should know, that the consequence of injustice is not merely lashes and death, which the wrong-doer sometimes escapes, but a punishment which is inevitable. For in the nature of things there are two types, namely one divine and blessed, the other ungodlike and repulsive; those who live unjustly do not see in the extremity of their folly and blindness that they are becoming like the earthly type and unlike the divine, and their reward is that their life is in harmony with the corresponding type or exemplar.

If we say to them that unless they abandon their unscrupulous ways they, when they die, will not be admitted into the place that is pure of evil, and in this world will be given over to things which are in conformity with their unworthy behavior, they in their abounding cunning and craft will look on us as giving the counsel of fools. However, one noteworthy thing befalls them. If they are willing to discuss in private their objections to philosophy, and wait manfully and unflinchingly to see the matter out, then, strange to say, they lose their satisfaction in themselves, their brilliant rhetoric fades, and they become as little children. But if these things are true, and the life of those who devote themselves to the acquisition and practice of Philosophy is more divine and felicitous than any other mode of living, we should do nothing else than to grasp nobly and ardently the principles of Philosophy.

XV. Truly, our natural condition, so far as education and ignorance are concerned, may be compared to a state of things like the following.[15] Imagine a number of men living in an underground cavernous chamber, with an entrance open to the light, extending along the entire length of the cavern, in which they have been confined from their childhood, with their legs and necks so shackled that they are obliged to sit still and look straight forward, because their chains render it impossible for them to turn their heads, and imagine a bright fire burning some way off, above and behind them,

15) Plato, *Republic*, 514A-517C.

and an elevated roadway passing between the fire and the prisoners, with a low wall built along it, like the screens which conjurers put up in front of their audience, and above which they exhibit their wonders. Moreover, figure a number of persons walking behind this wall, and carrying with them statues of men, and images of other animals, wrought in wood and stone and all kinds of materials, together with various other articles, which overtop the wall; and let some of the passers-by be talking and others silent.

This strange scene or image, and these strange prisoners, resemble us. For, in the first place, it is plain that persons so confined could not have seen anything of themselves or of each other beyond the shadows thrown by the fire upon the part of the cavern facing them, supposing that they were compelled all their lifetime to keep their heads unmoved. And, further, unquestionably their knowledge of the things carried past them is equally limited. Moreover, if they were able to converse with one another, that they would be in the habit of giving names to the shadows of things or objects which they saw before them. Again: if their prison-house returned an echo from the part facing them, whenever one of the passers-by opened his lips, doubtless they could refer the voice to nothing else than to the shadow which was passing. In this case beyond a doubt such persons would hold the shadows of those manufactured articles to be the only realities.

Now consider what would happen if the course of nature brought them a release from their fetters, and a remedy for their foolishness, in the following manner. Suppose that one of them has been released and compelled suddenly to stand up and turn his neck around and walk with open eyes toward the light; and suppose that he goes through all these actions with pain, and that the dazzling brilliance renders him incapable of discerning those objects of which he used formerly to see the shadows.

What answer could he be expected to make, if someone were to tell him that in those days he was watching foolish phantoms, but that now he is somewhat nearer to reality, and is turned toward things more real, and sees more correctly; above all, if he were to point out to him the several objects that are passing by, and question him, and force him to answer what they are? Certainly he would be puzzled, and regard his old visions as much truer than the objects now showed to him. And undoubtedly if he were further compelled to gaze at the light itself his eyes would be distressed, and he would shrink and turn away to the things which he could see distinctly, and consider them to be really clearer than the things pointed out to him.

Now if someone were to drag him violently up the rough and steep ascent from the cavern, and refuse to release him till he had drawn him out into the light of the sun, most certainly he would be vexed and indignant at such treatment and, on reaching the light, would find his eyes so dazzled by the glare as to be incapable of making out so much as one of the objects that are now called true. Therefore habit or custom will be necessary to enable him to perceive objects in that upper world. At first he will be most successful in distinguishing shadows; then he will discern the reflections of men and other things in water, and afterwards the realities; and after this he will raise his eyes to encounter the light of the moon and stars, finding it less difficult to study the heavenly bodies and the heaven itself by night than the sun and the sun's light by day. And, last of all, he will be able to observe and contemplate the nature of the sun, not as it appears in the water or on alien ground, but as it is in itself in its own territory. Next he will draw the conclusion that the sun is the author of the seasons and the years, and the guardian of all things in the visible world, and in a manner the cause of all those things which he and his companions used to see. Obviously he will proceed by these steps. The result is, that when he recollects his first habitation, and the wisdom of the place, and his old fellow-prisoners, he will assuredly congratulate himself on the change, and pity them. And if it was their practice in those days to receive honors and commendations one from another, and to give prizes to him who remembered best all that used to precede and follow and accompany events, and from these data divined most ably what was going to come next, it is evident that he will not covet these prizes, and envy those who receive honor and exercise authority among them. On the contrary, it is safe to say that he will feel what Homer describes, and wish extremely

As laborer to some ignoble man
To work for hire....[16]

and be ready to go through anything, rather than entertain those opinions and live in that fashion.

Now consider what would happen if such a man were to descend again and seat himself on his old place? Coming so suddenly out of the sun, he certainly would find his eyes blinded with the gloom of the place. And if he were forced to deliver his opinions again, touching the shadows aforesaid, and to enter the lists against those who had always been prisoners, while his sight continued dim, and his eyes were unsteady—and if this process of initiation lasted a considerable time—he unquestionably would be made a laughing-stock, and it would be said of him that he had gone up only to come back again with his eyesight destroyed, and that therefore it was not worthwhile even to attempt the ascent. And if anyone endeavored to set them free and carry them to the light, they would doubtless go so far as to put him to death, if they could only manage to get him into their power. This whole image must be referred to our former statements, by comparing the region which the eye reveals to the prison-house, and the light of the fire therein to the sun: and if, by the upward ascent and the contemplation of the upper world, we understand the ascending of the soul into the intellectual region, we will not miss the truth.

In the world of knowledge [the intelligible realm] the essential Form or Idea of the Good is the limit of our inquiries, and can scarcely be apprehended; but, when perceived, we must conclude that it is in every case the source of all that is right and beautiful—in the visible world giving birth to light and its master, and in the intellectual world dispensing, immediately and with full authority, truth and reason;—and that whosoever would act wisely, either in private or in public, must set this Idea of the Good before his eyes. If therefore this is the function and work of education, and it differs so greatly from ignorance, what other thing is it right for one to do than to acquire education and Philosophy, and those things which

16) Homer, *Odyssey*, 11, 489.

now appear to the multitude worthy of much attention to despise as contributing nothing worth mentioning to the acquiring of Felicity.

XVI.[17] Hence, if these things be true, we cannot avoid believing that the real nature of education is not such as some assert, who pretend to infuse into the mind a knowledge of which it was destitute, just as sight might be instilled into blinded eyes, whereas our present reasoning shows us that there is a power inherent in the soul of each person which is the instrument by which each of us is able to learn; and that just as we might suppose it to be impossible to turn the eye round from darkness to light without turning the whole body, so must this faculty or instrument be wheeled round in company with the entire soul away from the world of death and generation, until it is enabled to endure the contemplation of the real world and the brightest part of it, which we call the good. Hence this process of revolution or converting must give rise to an art teaching in what way the change will most easily and most effectually be brought about.[18] Its object will not be to implant in a person the power of seeing, but, on the contrary, it assumes that he possesses it, though he is turned in a wrong direction and does not look toward the right quarter; and its aim is to remedy this defect.

Therefore, though the other so-called virtues of the soul seem to resemble those of the body—inasmuch as they really do not preexist in the soul, but are formed in it in the course of time by habit and exercise—the virtue of wisdom does most certainly appertain to a more divine substance, which never loses its actuality, but by change of position becomes useful and serviceable, or else remains useless and injurious. For you must have noticed how keen-sighted are the puny souls of those who have the reputation of being clever but vicious, and how sharply they see through the things to which they are directed, thus proving that their powers of vision are by no

17) Plato, Republic, 518B-519B.

18) Sophist profess to put scientific knowledge into the soul; but Plato's argument indicates that the power or faculty of knowledge and its organ, Intellect, are already present in the soul of each individual, just as sight and eye are already possessed by the prisoners in the Cave. The doctrine that learning is reminiscence implies what is fundamentally the same view: see Meno, 81A, and Phædo, 72E-76D, especially 73A.

means feeble, though they have been compelled to become the
servants of wickedness, so that the more sharply they see, the more
numerous are the evils which they work. But, if from earliest
childhood these characters had been shorn and stripped of those
leaden, earth-born weights, which grow and cling to the pleasures
of eating, and gluttonous enjoyments of a similar nature, and which
keep the eye of the soul turned upon the things below—if they had
been released from these snares, and turned around to look at
objects that are true, then these very same souls of these very same
men would have had as keen an eye for such pursuits as they
actually have for those in which they are now engaged. Now,
therefore, since we are "born" here, it is evident from the same
reasoning what nature the function of Philosophy has and how
precious it is. *For to cleanse the soul of every taint of generation, and
to purify that actuality of it to which the power of reason belongs, is
the chief function of Philosophy.* This therefore is the best mode of
living, namely to live and die practicing justice and the other
virtues: and this mode we must follow, if we wish to become truly
happy.

XVII. But if our hearers should be advised from ancient discourses and sacred myths, both of the Pythagoreans and others,
from these we will proceed to draw an exhortation. Rightly are
those called happy who need nothing, and the life of those who have
innumerable desires is dangerous and full of trouble.[19] I should not
wonder, indeed, if Euripides is right when he says,

> Who knoweth if to live is to be dead,
> And to be dead is to live?[20]

And one might wonder if we are all really dead, and the body is our
tomb, and that part of the soul in which the desires reside is of a
nature liable to be over-persuaded and to be swayed continually to
and fro. And so some smart Sicilian or Italian turned this into a

19) Iamblichus here follows Plato, *Gorgias*, 493ff.
20) Polyidus, fragment 7.

fable, and, playing with the word, from its susceptibility to all impressions and capacity for holding belief, named it a jar, and the foolish he called uninitiated: in these uninitiated, that part of the soul where the desires are, the licentious and non-retentive portion of it, he compared to a jar full of holes, because there was no possibility of filling or satisfying it. Wherefore, this thinker shows, contrary to the opinion of the multitude, that of all those in Hades, which signifies the invisible region, the uninitiated are the most miserable, and are forced to carry water into their leaky jar in a sieve perforated just like the other. And by the sieve he represents the soul: and the soul of the foolish he likened to a sieve, because it is full of holes, as incapable of holding anything by reason of its incredulity and forgetfulness, i.e., its inaptitude for receiving and retaining knowledge. This may indeed seem somewhat whimsical; still it shows clearly what I want to prove, namely that one should choose, in preference to a life of insatiable self-indulgence, one that is orderly and regular and ever content and satisfied with what it has.

I will give you another illustration from the same source. Consider, if you allow something of this kind to be a representation of each of the two lives, the life of self-control and of self-indulgence, as it might be if of two men each had several jars, and those of one were sound and full, one of wine and another of honey and a third of milk, and a number of others full of various things of which there were streams scanty and hard to get at and procurable only by many severe toils. He whose jars are full draws no more and troubles himself no more about the matter, but as far as this is concerned remains quite at his ease: but the other finds, like the former, the streams possible though difficult to come at, and his vessels weak and decayed, and is forced to be constantly filling them all day and all night or else be a prey to the most excruciating pains. If such therefore be the nature of each of these two lives, do you maintain that that of the self-indulgent or intemperate man is happier than that of the regular and orderly and temperate? For the life of one consists in this, in the influx of as much as possible, in which case, then, the more you pour in the greater the waste—

wide too must be the holes for the liquid to escape by;[21] which is nothing else than to live a life like that of an obscene and ravenous bird: but the life of the other being filled once for all with his own goods remains contented through all time. Such is a certain ancient exhortation to the study of Virtue.

XVIII. Cognate to this there is another way, which by analogy from those things which are clear and conspicuous in the body passes to the evils and goods of the soul, which, diverting our will and pursuit from the evil, and making us alien as it were to the base and degrading, exhorts us to grasp the good with all our strength, and to bring our mind in every way into an association with the good: so that if we must fly from the passions and maladies of the body, much more must we avoid those of the soul. Injustice, which is a disease of the soul, is intolerable to him who is afflicted with it. Now, if the body is unsymmetrically constituted it injures the perfection of our soul to such an extent that when that by which we live is in a vicious condition and discordant within itself, it is not possible to live rightly. But let us consider each of these from the same standpoint.[22] For just as our bodies work well when they have order and harmony, but badly when they lack order, so likewise the soul lacking order will be evil, but good having order and harmony: and that which arises in the body from order and harmony is called

---

21) The meaning of this Pythagorean myth is as follows: We are said to be dead because the soul partakes of inanimation. The sepulchre which we carry about with us is, as Plato himself says, the body. But Hades is the invisible or obscure, because we are situated in obscurity, the soul being in a condition of servitude to the body. The jars are the desires, which are so called either from the hastening to fill them as if they were jars, or from desire persuading us that it is beautiful. The initiated, therefore, i.e. those who have a perfect knowledge, pour into the entire jar: for these have their jar full, i.e. they have perfect virtue. But the uninitiated, namely those who possess nothing perfect, have perforated jars. For those who are slaves to desire always wish to fill it, and are more excited, and on this account they have perforated jars, as being never full. But the sieve is the rational soul mingled with the irrational. For the soul is called a circle because it seeks itself and is itself sought; it finds itself, and is itself found. But the irrational soul imitates a right line since it does not return to itself like a circle. Insofar as the sieve is circular it is an image of the rational soul but, as it is placed under the right lines formed from the holes, it is assumed for the irrational soul. Right lines, therefore, are in the middle of the cavities. Hence by 'the sieve' Plato signifies the rational in subjection to the irrational soul. The water is the flux of nature for, as Heraclitus says, moisture is the death of the soul.—Olympiodorus.

22) Plato, Gorgias, 504A-505B.

health and strength; and that which is engendered in the soul from the same is named lawfulness and law. For just as we call the right condition of the body "healthy," whence it is that health is produced in it and every other corporeal excellence—so the order in the soul is called law by which also men are made observant of law and orderly; and these are justice and temperance. So, therefore, it is to this that the man of science and virtue will have regard in applying to men's souls whatsoever words he addresses to them, and will conform all his actions; and if he give any gift he will give, or if he take aught away he will take it, with his mind always intent on this, namely how to implant justice in the souls of his fellow citizens and eradicate injustice, to engender temperance and extirpate intemperance, to engender all other virtues and remove all vice. For what can be the advantage of offering to a sick and diseased boy a quantity of the nicest things to eat and drink or anything else when, fairly considered, they will do him no more good sometimes than the contrary, or even less? Such is the case.

I judge that it is no advantage to a man to live with his body in a vicious condition, since in that case his life also must be a miserable and vicious one. And so, again, when a man is in health, the physicians for the most part allow him to gratify his appetite, as for instance, to eat as much as he pleases when he is hungry or drink when he is thirsty, but a sick man they never, so to speak, allow to indulge his appetites to the full. And the same reasoning will apply to the soul. For so long as the soul is in a vicious condition, foolish and unjust and impious, we must prevent it from indulging its appetites, and not suffer it to do anything except that which will make it better: for this course is better for the soul itself. Therefore the restraining a man from the gratification of his sensuous desires is a punishment. Punishment or restraint therefore is better for the soul than *unrestrained* self-indulgence or the gratification of licentious desires, as even the multitude think, and the condition of being temperate and harmonious is to be much preferred to that of being intemperate and inordinate. Wherefore in every way justice and temperance must be cultivated and practiced instead of the contrary habits. And let this be our statement on the subject.

XIX. Truly one would be able to discuss the question at issue separately from the goods which are in the soul, showing what is perfect in them and the characteristic property of Felicity. For as much as the soul excels the body so much likewise do its goods surpass those of the body; and those of the body should be despised, indeed, but those of the soul should be deemed most precious and honorable. Good therefore is not the same as pleasure, and pleasure is not to be pursued for the sake of the good, nor good for the sake of pleasure: that is pleasant which brings pleasure by its presence, and that good which by its presence makes us good. We, indeed, and everything else that is good, have that character by the acquisition of some virtue. But the virtue of anything, whether it be of an instrument, or of body, or of soul, or of any living creature whatsoever, cannot be acquired best by accident; it must be due to that particular order and rightness and art which is assigned severally to each of them. Wherefore the virtue of everything implies order and harmonious arrangement, as one would say who reasoned rightly. In everything accordingly it is by the introduction of some kind of order, namely that which is proper to each, that this is in every case made good: therefore a soul also when it has its own proper order and harmony is better than one devoid of order. And one which is endowed with order is orderly; and the orderly soul is temperate; and the temperate soul is good.

I say, therefore, that if the temperate soul is good, the soul which is in a condition directly opposed to temperance is evil: and this is none other than the insensate and dissolute soul. This indeed must of necessity be so. Further, the [temperate] man of sound mind will do what is right toward Gods and men: for it must necessarily be that no man could be sound in mind if he did the contrary. And, again, when he does what is right and proper toward men, his actions will be just, and toward the Gods pious; but a man who does what is just and pious must necessarily be a just and pious man. Moreover, he must be brave, too: for certainly temperance or self-control consists not in pursuing or avoiding what one ought not, but in pursuing and avoiding what one ought, whether things or men, or pleasures or pains, and in steadfast endurance at the call of duty. Wherefore it is entirely necessary that the temperate man, as we have shown, being just and brave and pious has attained the perfection of goodness, and that the good man does well and fairly all that he does, and that he who does well is blessed and happy, and the bad man and evil doer is miserable: and this must be the man who is in the opposite condition of mind to the temperate, namely the licentious. Wherefore, it this be true, every one who wishes to be happy must seek after and practice self-control, and flee from licentiousness as fast as his feet will carry him, and so act that he will not need punishment; but if he should require it, either himself or any of those connected with him, be it individual or state, then justice and correction must be applied if he is to have any chance of happiness.

This seems to me to be the mark on which a man should fix his gaze through life; to that he should bend all his powers and all the powers of the state, and so act that Justice and Temperance shall be his portion, as they must be if he would be truly happy—not letting his desires grow without restraint and so in the attempt to satisfy them find a never ending evil and torment, leading the life of a robber. For neither to any other man can such a one be dear, nor to God; for he is incapable of fellowship, and with one in whom there is no fellowship, friendship is impossible. And the wise tell us that the heaven and the earth, and Gods and men, are kept together by fellowship and friendship and orderliness and temperance and justice, and this is why they give the name of "order" (*cosmos*) to the universe and not of disorder or license. But he who has paid no attention to these things, has overlooked the mighty power of geometrical equality in heaven as well as in earth.[23] Hence they think that a spirit of inequality, the desire of obtaining more than one's fair share, should be cultivated, because they neglect geometry. And such therefore is the universal reason or law of a life of felicity. And it may be added that they preferred to die nobly to whom it was not permitted to live honorably and well, rather than subject their children and posterity to infamy, and reflect shame and dishonor upon their parents and forefathers. For the life of one who dishonors his race is not worth living, and such a man can have no friend either upon the earth among mankind, or among the Gods

23) Plato, *Gorgias*, 507E.

in the realms beneath.[24]

Every man, therefore, if he aims to do anything, should act with virtue, knowing that without virtue all possessions and pursuits are base and infamous. For wealth can bring no honor to an unmanly or cowardly mind: the riches of such a person are for others, not for himself. Nor must beauty and strength of body, when dwelling in a base and cowardly man, be deemed ornamental, but disgraceful: since they make the possessor more conspicuous, and show forth his cowardice. Moreover, knowledge, when separated from justice and the other virtues, is not wisdom but cunning: wherefore make it your first and last and all-absorbing aim to surpass our ancestors in glory, but, if this cannot be done, at least to equal them in uprightness. For victory in this contest brings honor; defeat brings infamy. The most effectual way to win this victory is so to order your conduct and life as not to abuse or waste the reputation of our ancestors, knowing that to a man who has any self-respect, nothing is more dishonorable than to be honored not for his own sake but on account of the reputation of his ancestors. The honor or reputation indeed of parents is a noble and magnificent treasury; but to have the use of a treasury of wealth and honor, and to leave none to your successors, because you have neither money nor reputation of your own, is alike base and dishonorable. For from himself every one should make a beginning in the acquisition of all goods and of those things which lead to glory and felicity. For the ancient proverb,[25] "nothing too much," was well said. For he whose happiness rests with himself alone—who is not hanging in suspense on other men, or changing with the vicissitude of their fortune—has his life ordered for the best. He is temperate and valiant and wise; and when his riches come and go, when his children are given and taken away, he will remember and obey the ancient proverb, "neither rejoicing overmuch nor grieving overmuch," for he relies upon himself. And such we wish the good to be, not lamenting overmuch if they should die at the present time, or suffer any other of human ills. *For one should firmly and always*

24) Plato, *Menexenus*, 246D-247B.
25) Plato, *Menexenus*, 247E-248B.

believe that the good man,[26] *because he is temperate and just, is fortunate and happy; and he is so whether he be great and strong or small and weak, and whether he be rich or poor: but the unjust man, even though he is richer than Cinyras*[27] *or Midas, is wretched and lives in misery.*

Therefore the poet says, and truly: "I sing not, I care not about him who accomplishes all noble things, not having justice," let him who "draws near and stretches out his hand against his enemies be a just man." But if he be unjust, I would not have him "look calmly upon bloody death," nor "surpass in swiftness the Thracian Boreas;" and let no other thing that is called good ever be his.

For the "goods" of which the many speak are not really good: for they put first health, beauty next, wealth third; and then innumerable others, as, for example, to have a keen eye or a quick ear, and in general to have all the senses perfect; or, again, to be a tyrant and do as you like; and the summit of all beatitude, in the opinion of the many, is to have acquired all these things, and when you have acquired them to become at once immortal. But I affirm, without qualification, that while to the just and holy all these things are the best of possessions, to the unjust they are all, including even health, the greatest of evils. For in truth to have sight, and hearing, and the use of the senses, or to live at all without justice and virtue, even though a man be rich in all the so-called goods of fortune, is the greatest of evils, if life here be immortal, but not so great if the bad man lives only a very short time. For I positively declare that evils as they are termed are goods to the unjust, and only evil to the just; and that goods are truly good to the good but evil to the evil. And he who lives unjustly and insolently will of necessity live basely, but if basely, evilly, and therefore painfully, and to his own disadvantage. For if we affirm as from the Gods that the just life is the most pleasant, we will speak most truly. *If therefore goods are inherent in the life according to virtue, and in that alone, then the things that are truly good and pure joy accompany the philosopher alone.* For the sake therefore of all these, those who desire to become truly

---

26) Plato, Laws, 660E-662A.
27) A son of Apollo and King of Cyprus, proverbially wealthy.

happy choose a virtuous life.

XX. I think, therefore, that the exhortation by admonitions or counsels is not out of place here, and that it is as it were united to the precept which directs the right manner of living, and that it especially shows that the parts of the discourse inciting to the study of Philosophy are not disconnected, but that all are in harmony with each other. In accordance with this conception therefore we will begin from the most excellent precept, namely that we should practice piety. But this cannot be done unless he who worships becomes similar to that which is worshipped. But nothing else than Philosophy can effect this similitude.

It is especially necessary to state the truth about a matter of great importance. For to speak the truth, both in reference to the Gods in divine things and in reference to men in human things, leads us to all goods both human and divine. But truth being of such a character comes through Philosophy alone, for philosophers alone are lovers of truth. Moreover, it is right that all should know the power of the laws, and how this power may be useful to them. But it is not possible to learn this unless we know and practice virtue, to the similitude of which we may recall the power and use of the laws. But the cultivation or practice of virtue arises by means of philosophy: so that to this we come by the guidance of Philosophy.

Moreover, it is necessary to know how we should associate with men. But this no one will know unless he investigates and discovers what is fitting or right in all actions, and knows what should be attributed and what not attributed to different men and is able to perceive the customs or habits and natures of different men, and the powers of the soul, and the discourses adapted to all of these. But none of these can be acquired without the aid of philosophy, and therefore on account of these it will be most useful.

But if the law of manliness commands that we should both resist brutal or savage men and master the most dangerous animals, and should meet dangers intrepidly and accustom ourselves to endure them—let us see in reference to these things what science provides as useful for this purpose. This will be no other than philosophy alone, in my opinion. For philosophy practices diligently the endurance and contempt of death, cultivates through the whole of life self-control, bears and meets labors and difficulties nobly, and wholly despises pleasures. Wherefore philosophy alone should those seek and apprehend who wish to participate in all divine and human goods. In sum, whatever one may wish to do, in order that he may reach the greatest perfection, either by wisdom, fortitude, eloquence, or virtue, either as a whole or any part thereof—by any or all of these aids he will be able to accomplish his purpose.

First he must be "born" and for his "birth" he is indebted to fortune: but certain things are forthwith in the power of man—such as, for instance, that he may become desirous of things beautiful and good, a lover of labor, and that he may apply himself to the acquisition of knowledge early in life and continue to learn for a long period of time. But if one of these is absent he will not be able to reach the highest end, but having all these he will become so perfect in that which he practices and cultivates that he will be unsurpassable. But if this is true in respect to other sciences, how much more must it be so in respect to the most excellent of all arts, Philosophy? For the sake of this all labors should be cheerfully undertaken and endured, much time spent in learning, and the greatest ardor in acquiring it manifested.

In addition to this, if at any particular time one wishes to gain reputation among men, and to be valued for his true character, he must begin from his youth to work for these objects continuously and persistently, and not at odd intervals. For if to the attainment of any of these objects one has been devoted for a long time, and has cultivated it from the first to the end, he will acquire a substantial reputation and fame because he is now trusted indubitably; and the envy of man is not excited on account of which they do not extol nor mention with praise some things, and other things they condemn falsely and unjustly. For it is not agreeable to men to specially honor another man who is superior to them, for they think that by so doing they deprive themselves of a certain good: but forced by necessity, and influenced little by little for a long time, they praise though most grudgingly: and at the same time they do not doubt whether a man is really such as he appears to be, or whether he hunts for and secures praise through false pretenses, and deceives men by giving an honest appearance to those things which he does.

For in the way to which I have already referred, he who practices virtue produces faith in it, and gains a reputation for himself.

Subdued by facts men neither are able to indulge in envy any longer, nor believe any longer that they are deceived. Moreover, the effort and long time spent on each work and deed confirms by reason of the long time that which is practiced: a short time will not do this. And in the art of speaking, if one has learned it thoroughly, in a short time he will not be inferior to his teacher; but the virtue which arises from many good deeds one cannot acquire in perfection if he begins late, nor in a short time, but it is necessary that he grow and be matured with it, abstaining from evil acts and habits, but giving much care and attention to the cultivation and practice of the contraries of these. But in a short time censure will be attached to fame or reputation. For those who suddenly and quickly become either rich or wise or good or brave—these rapid achievements other men do not receive gladly. But if we say these things truly, it is not possible that we can obtain a similitude of habits, constant and irrefragable, otherwise than through Philosophy alone: and it will appear clearly from the premises, that, if we wish to become perfectly good and acquire true glory and felicity, we must do nothing else than philosophize. Moreover, this counsel leads to the same end, that when one desires anything he must pursue this to the utmost, whether it be eloquence or wisdom or strength, and this acquirement should be used for a good purpose and in accordance with the laws. But if one uses the present good for an unjust purpose, and illegally, such conduct is the worst of all, and the good is better absent than present: and just as he is perfectly good who, if he possesses any of these goods, uses them rightly, so, on the contrary, he is perfectly evil who uses them badly. And we must deem him who aims at all virtue to become the best, by reason of the fact that he is useful to most.

If one by giving money aids his neighbors, the indigent, he will be forced to become evil, since, having consumed his wealth by donations, he will not be able to collect additional riches of such a magnitude that they will never be exhausted. [Therefore if one is unable to donate more he will be bad, if Virtue consists in mere giving.] Moreover, after the accumulation of wealth a second evil will arise, if from being rich he becomes poor, and from possessing lacks everything. How therefore will one who benefits mankind, not by distributing wealth but in some other way, and this not with evil but with virtue, be able to do this—and how if he is generous with his donations will he never lack the means to make them? This he will be able to do, if he is aided and directed by justice and the laws. For justice is the connecting bond of states and men, and the foundation of government itself.

Again, from the following consideration the same conclusions may be drawn. For if Philosophy genuinely gives the right use of all things in life, and the distribution of intellect which we call Law, those wishing to participate in the perfect life should do nothing else than truly philosophize. And indeed every man ought to have a perfect mastery of himself. But one will especially possess this, if he is superior to wealth, by which all are corrupted, and his soul is strenuously devoted to the apprehension and practice of justice and virtue, for in the pursuit of these many are weak. Wherefore they incur this censure, that they are lovers of the soul because life and the soul are the same; and that therefore they use carefully and desire it on account of the love and habit of life, by which they are nourished, but they love wealth in order to guard against those things which terrify them. But what are these? Diseases, old age, and sudden losses or penalties. I do not refer to the penalties inflicted by the laws, for these may be expected and avoided, but those such as fires, deaths of domestic animals, and other calamities which befall—some of the body, some of the soul, and others of worldly goods. On account of all these things, therefore, every man desires wealth in order that when any of these misfortunes befall him, he may repair his losses.

And there are other things which equally, as said before, incite men to the pursuit and acquisition of wealth, such as competition with each other, business vocations and power, on account of which they consider wealth of great importance, because it is the product of these things. But the man who is truly good does not seek fame clothed with an alien garment but with his own virtue [worth]. And hence, since philosophy is the cause of all goods, and calls us from the passions and the use of external things, it will be the most useful of all in aiding us to reach a happy life.

And concerning the love of life: one should be persuaded that, if it was given to man because, unless he was killed by another or by disease he would be exempt from old age and immortal during the rest of time, then it would be easy to excuse or justify him who preserves life; but since extreme old age is an evil to men, and since there is no earthly immortality, and since great ignorance and depravity of speech and actions and desires flourish, there is no excuse for him who aims to preserve indefinitely the mere physical life, and it is plain that the mass of men would prefer to preserve this mortal life with all its infamies rather than to exchange it for an eternal and ever-living life of felicity.[28]

If therefore Philosophy alone inspires meditation and contempt of death, and leads to the immortal and eternal life, and imparts to us a knowledge of the eternal productive principles or Ideas, and accustoms us to imitate these, then on account of these benefits, also, it is the most useful and practical of all things. Moreover, we should not encourage people in greed and selfishness, nor should power in connection with arrogance be considered a virtue, nor obedience to laws as timidity. For this conception of things is the worst, and from it spring all things contrary to good, namely evil and calamity. For if men are so constituted by nature that they are not able to live alone but associate with each other, yielding to necessity, and for the sake of and in reference to this association all life is regulated, and all arts were invented by them, neither can society exist without the government of law, for the absence of law would bring a greater disadvantage and penalty to them than a solitary life—wherefore, by reason of these necessary causes, law and justice rule among men, and these are in nowise changed or become extinct, for they are permanent by nature.

If one, therefore, should have from the beginning such a nature that his body was invulnerable and exempt from diseases and other evils, and he was adamantine in both body and soul, to such a one perhaps power in connection with arrogance and superiority might seem sufficient—for such a one violating the laws would be able to

28) This passage, like many others in Iamblichus, is corrupt.

escape unpunished. But not rightly does a man of this kind reason. For if there should be one of this kind, who was not an ally of the laws and justice, and did not strengthen them and use his power in aid of these and their followers—in thus acting such a one would be temporarily safe, but otherwise he would not be able to secure himself from punishment and injury. For all would think that by their obedience to the laws they became the enemies of a man of this kind, and a multitude would defeat him by artifice or by power, and conquer him. Thus it appears that force itself, if it is really power, is preserved by law and justice. But, apart from these considerations, the just is to be chosen of and for itself, and we are naturally disposed to cultivate and acquire it. Therefore if even nothing of external goods results from the practice of justice, or if even certain human losses or disasters befall, we must still act justly, since this is most important and precious to all.

One should learn about law and anarchy, so far as they differ from each other, and should know that the rule of law is the best both privately and publicly, but that the reign of anarchy is the worst. For crimes and injuries forthwith arise from anarchy. But we will first note those things which arise from the rule of law. Faith in our fellow-men first arises, which is of the greatest utility to all men, and ranks among the greatest goods. For by reason of it goods become common, and even though they may be few, they suffice when they are evenly distributed. Without this faith they would not suffice, even though they were many. And the contingencies of fortune which are concerned with wealth and life, both profitable and unprofitable, legal and illegal, are governed by men through law. For the happy are safe and not disturbed by malignant fortune, but the unhappy on the contrary are aided by the happy through intercourse and faith which come from obedience to and confidence in the supremacy of the moral law. Therefore the time spent in the study and practice of justice or equity is empty of disputes and troubles, but that consumed otherwise is productive of contentions.

Men who dwell in obedience to law are liberated from most unpleasant trouble, and live most agreeably. For the trouble or annoyance of contentions or litigations is most unpleasant, but the performance of equitable deeds most pleasant. They simply dream who imagine that there will be a cessation of evils to men, and that without fear and sorrow they will attain the object of their thoughts and care; and that, securing this, they will enjoy things of a similar kind—but those who live rightly do not arise terrified with a sudden fear, nor do they arise because they know that a pleasing condition must be exchanged for the day, but they arise contentedly and untroubled, applying themselves to the affairs of life, but they alleviate their labors by well-founded and expected hopes of acquiring the goods of life—of all which the study and practice of equity or justice is the cause.

And even that which is productive of the greatest evils to men, war, brings more destruction and slavery to those who disdain the laws than to those who are law-abiding.

And indeed many other goods which bring alleviations and protection to life and a consolation for hardships arise from the study and practice of justice or equity.

From anarchy, on the contrary, arise these evils. First, it gives to men no leisure for good works; they [the lawless] devote themselves to the most odious things but not to good deeds, and through treachery and illiberality they hoard up wealth, but it is not used for the public benefit, and thus though there may be an abundance of things a scarcity of them arises. The contingencies of fortune, both good and bad, serve contrary purposes: for prosperity is not safe when anarchy reigns, but is insidiously undermined; and adversity is not driven away or expelled but is strengthened by treachery and ferocity.

External war and domestic sedition arise often from the same cause, and if not before then this happens when men plot treacherously against each other, and shunning each other, engage in a continuous counter-plotting. But neither do the wakeful experience agreeable thought, nor is there to those immersed in sleep a pleasant couch, but they are agitated by fear and the sudden recollection of evils—all of which evils, and the others before noted, arise from anarchy.

But tyranny, which is so great and such an evil, comes from no other source than anarchy. Some men think, but not rightly, that a tyrant originates from another cause, and that men are deprived of their liberty not by themselves, but that they are forcibly deprived of it by the tyrant, but this reasoning is invalid. For whoever thinks that a king or tyrant arises from anything but anarchy and greed is foolish. For when all are engaged in evil pursuits then a ruler must arise: for it is not possible for men to live without law and justice. But when law and justice have departed from the multitude, then the care and custody of these will pass into the hands of someone. For how otherwise can the government be transferred to one except by the expulsion of law, which is profitable to and preservative of the multitude? For it is necessary that the man who overthrows justice and subverts the law, which is common and beneficial to all, be adamantine if he is able to strip these from the multitude of men, being himself one of the multitude: but he is of flesh and like other men, and therefore not able to do this, but, on the contrary, restoring them when they have been cast aside, he alone will rule. But this fact some have not discovered.

If therefore anarchy is the cause of such great evils, and order is the cause of such great goods, it is not possible otherwise to acquire felicity unless one constitutes law as the guide of his whole life. But this is right reason perceiving and directing what is to be done and prohibiting things that should not be done, both in the universe and in states and in private houses, and in every individual in reference to his own conduct. *If therefore this reason dealing with goods and evils, with beautiful and base things, cannot be learned in any other way, and when it is learned cannot be followed, except by philosophizing perfectly, for the sake of these philosophy must be cultivated and practiced above all other human pursuits or studies.*

XXI. The last mode of exhortation to virtue is that based on symbols, one way being peculiar to the Pythagorean school and sacred compared with other institutions, another popular and common to other schools, and the third a mediate between the other two, being neither entirely popular nor entirely Pythagorean, but not wholly different from the others. Of such as are called Pythagoric symbols, those which are worthy of commemoration and appear to have a special exhortative power, we will impart with an appropriate interpretation, believing that in this way we will give to our readers a full and more perfect exhortation to Philosophy than they would get if it was expounded more voluminously. So far, therefore, as we may give some exoteric solutions or interpretations common to all philosophy, these must be understood to be different from the Pythagorean signification: but to the extent that we introduce some of the principal opinions of these men about particular symbols, so far again this is peculiar to the Pythagoreans, and entirely different from other philosophers, rightly considered. This method will imperceptibly lead us from the exoteric opinions, bringing us to and making us acquainted with the others, and to the exhortations constructed according to the Pythagorean school, which are as it were a bridge or ladder by which we ascend upward from below, and to a height from a depth, attracting and guiding the minds of all who genuinely apply themselves to the work. For to this end or purpose these symbols were devised, according to an imitation and expression of the things previously declared.

For the most ancient thinkers, and those who were contemporary with and disciples of Pythagoras himself, did not compose their writings in a common and popular stye, and in a manner usual with all other writers, intelligible and easy to be understood offhand, as if they were attempting to make their conceptions easy of apprehension—but, in accordance with the silence about the Mysteries, prescribed by Pythagoras as a law, they used modes recondite and unintelligible to the uninitiated, and concealed from others through symbols their thoughts and discourses. And therefore unless one who apprehends these symbols unfolds their meaning by a lucid interpretation they will seem to those who may meet with them to be ridiculous and inane, and full of nugacity and garrulity—[but, being rightly explained, and instead of dark made obvious and clear even to the multitude, then they will be found analogous to prophetic sayings, and to the oracles of the Pythian Apollo. They will then also disclose an admirable meaning, and will produce a divine inspiration in those who unite intellect with erudition].[29]

In order therefore that the great utility of these symbols may be

29) Iamblichus, *Life of Pythagoras*, chapter 23.

known, and their exhortative use may be manifest, we will give the solution or interpretation of every symbol, according to both the exoteric and oral modes of transmission, not omitting those things which were preserved in silence and not communicated to the uninitiated.

The following are the Symbols which will be elucidated:

1. Entering a temple worship, meanwhile neither say nor do anything which pertains to ordinary life.

2. Enter not into a temple negligently, nor, in brief, adore carelessly, not even though you should stand at the very doors themselves.

3. Sacrifice and adore unshod.

4. Disbelieve nothing amazing concerning the Gods or divine dogmas.

5. Leaving the public ways, walk in unfrequented paths.

6. Abstain from Melanurus, for it belongs to the terrestrial Gods.

7. Above all things, govern your tongue when you follow the Gods.

8. When the winds blow, worship the sound.

9. Cut not fire with a sword.

10. Turn away from yourself every sharp edge.

11. Help a man to take up a burden, but not to lay it down.

12. Put the shoe on the right foot first, but put the left foot first into the bath tub.

13. Speak not about Pythagoric concerns without light.

14. Pass not over a pair of scales. [Do not step above the beam of the balance].

15. Traveling from home turn not back, for the Furies will go back with you.

16. Do not urinate facing the sun.

17. Clean not a seat with a torch.

18. Nourish a cock, but do not sacrifice it, for it is sacred to the sun and the moon.

19. Do not sit upon a choenix [bushel].

20. Nourish nothing which has crooked talons or nails.

21. Cut not in the way.

22. Do not receive a swallow into your house.

23. Do not wear a ring.

24. Inscribe not the image of God on a ring.

25. Look not in a mirror by lamp-light.

26. Do not indulge in immoderate laughter.

27. Do not pare your nails while sacrificing.

28. Do not readily seize everyone with your right hand.

29. When you rise from bed disorder the covering, and efface the impression of the body.

30. Eat not the heart.

31. Eat not the brain.

32. Spit upon the cuttings of your hair and the parings of your nails.

33. Do not receive the fish Erythrinus.

34. Destroy the print of a pot in the ashes.

35. Draw not near to that which has gold, in order to produce children.

36. Honor more a figure and step than a figure and three obols.

37. Abstain from beans.

38. Transplant mallows in your garden, but eat them not.

39. Abstain from the use of living creatures.

All these symbols are in general exhortative to all virtue; and each of them in particular leads to some particular virtue. And to parts of Philosophy and disciplinary learning different symbols are differently adapted—as, for instance, the first are directly exhortative to piety and divine science.

Symbol 1

This, *entering a temple worship, meanwhile neither say nor do anything which pertains to ordinary life,* signifies that one should preserve the divine as in and of itself, unmingled and undefiled, uniting the pure to the pure, and taking care lest anything of human affairs intrudes itself into the divine worship: for all these things are totally alien and antagonistic to it. Moreover, this conduces much to the acquisition of science: for to the divine science should be brought no such thing as human opinion or care of the external life. Nothing else therefore is commanded by this precept than that divine discourses and sacred actions should not be blended with the unstable and weak manners and habits of men.

Symbol 2

To the first is consonant the second, *enter not into a temple negligently, nor, in brief, adore carelessly, not even though you should stand at the very doors themselves.* For if the similar is friendly and allied to the similar, it is evident that, since the Gods have a most principal essence among wholes, we ought to make the worship of them a principal object. But he who does this for the sake of anything else gives a secondary rank to that which takes the precedency of all things, and subverts the whole order of religious worship and knowledge. Besides, it is not proper to rank illustrious goods in the subordinate condition of human utility, nor to place our concerns in the order of an end but things more excellent, whether they be works or conceptions, in the condition of an appendage.

Symbol 3

To the same end is the exhortation from the next symbol, *sacrifice and adore unshod.* For this signifies that we ought to worship the Gods and acquire a knowledge of them in an orderly and modest manner, and in a way not exceeding the order established on the earth. It also signifies that in worshipping them, and acquiring this knowledge, we should be free from bonds, and properly liberated. But this symbol exhorts that sacrifice and adoration should be performed not only in the body, but also in the activities of the soul; so that these activities may neither be fettered by passions, nor by the imbecility of the body, nor by generation with which we are externally surrounded. But every thing pertaining to us should be properly liberated and prepared for an association with the Gods.

Symbol 4

The next symbol, *disbelieve nothing amazing concerning the Gods, or divine dogmas,* is similar, exhorting to the acquisition of the same virtue. For this dogma sufficiently venerates and unfolds the transcendency of the Gods, affording us a viaticum, and recalls to our memory that we ought not to estimate divine power by our judgment. But it is likely that some things should appear difficult and impossible to us, in consequence of our corporeal subsistence, and from our association with generation and corruption; from our having a momentary existence; from being subject to a variety of diseases; from the smallness of our habitation; from our gravitating tendency to the middle; from our somnolency, indigence, and repletion; from our want of counsel and our imbecility; from the impediments of our soul, and a variety of other circumstances, although our nature possesses many illustrious prerogatives. At the same time, however, we perfectly fall short of the Gods, and possess neither the same power with them nor equal virtue.

This symbol therefore in a particular manner introduces the knowledge of the Gods, as beings who are able to affect all things. On this account it exhorts us to disbelieve nothing concerning the Gods. It also adds, "nor about divine dogmas," namely those belonging to the Pythagoric philosophy. For these being secured by disciplines and scientific theory are alone true and free from falsehood, being corroborated by all-various demonstration, accompanied with necessity. The same symbol, moreover, is capable of exhorting us to the science concerning the Gods: for it urges us to acquire a science of that kind, through which we shall be in no respect deficient in things asserted about the Gods. It is also able to exhort the same things concerning divine dogmas, and a disciplinative progression. For disciplines alone give eyes to and produce light about all things in him who intends to consider and survey them. For from the participation of disciplines one thing before all others is effected, namely a belief in the nature, essence, and power of the Gods, and also in those Pythagoric dogmas which appear to be marvelous to such as have not been introduced to and are uninitiated in disciplines: so that the precept, *disbelieve nothing,* is equivalent to *participate in and acquire* those things through which you will not disbelieve; that is to say, acquire disciplines and scientific demonstrations.

Symbol 5

I think that this symbol, *leaving the public ways, walk in unfrequented paths,* contributes to the same thing as the preceding. For this exhorts us to abandon a popular and merely human life, but commands us to pursue a separate and divine life. It also signifies that it is necessary to look above common opinions, but very much to esteem such as are private and arcane; and that we should despise merely human delight, but ardently pursue that felicitous mode of conduct which adheres to the divine will. It likewise exhorts us to dismiss human manners as popular, and to exchange for these the religious cultivation of the Gods, as transcending a popular life.

Symbol 6

Cognate to the preceding is the sixth symbol, *abstain from Melanurus,*[30] *for it belongs to the terrestrial Gods.* This admonishes us to enter upon the celestial journey, to unite ourselves to the intellectual Gods, to become separate from a material nature, and to be led as it were in a circular progression to an immaterial and pure life. It further exhorts us to adopt the most excellent worship of the Gods, and especially that which pertains to the primary Gods. This symbol therefore exhorts us to the knowledge and worship of the Gods, but the following symbol exhorts us to wisdom.

Symbol 7

Above all things govern your tongue, when you follow the Gods. For the primary work of wisdom is the converting of the dianoetic power or discursive reason to itself, and to accustom it not to proceed externally, but to be perfected within itself, both in the conversion to itself and, after this, in following the Gods. For nothing so perfects the intellect as, when it is converted to itself, to follow the Gods.

Symbol 8

When the winds blow, worship the sound. This is a sign of divine wisdom: for it intimates that we should love the imitation of or becoming similar to the divine essences and powers, and when their words accord with their activities to honor and reverence them with

30) According to Ælian and Suidas, Melanurus is a fish; but as the word signifies that which has a black termination, it is very appropriately used as a symbol of a material nature.— Bridgman.

the greatest zeal.

Symbol 9

Cut not fire with a sword. This exhorts to wisdom. For it excites in us an appropriate conception with respect to the propriety of not opposing sharp words to a man full of fire and wrath, nor contending with him. For frequently by words you will agitate and disturb an ignorant man, and will yourself experience things dreadful and unpleasant. Heraclitus also testifies to the truth of this symbol, saying: "It is difficult to fight with anger: for whatever anger desires to be done it will gain if possible, even at the cost of life." And this he says truly: for many by gratifying anger have changed the condition of their soul, and made death preferable to life. But by governing the tongue, and being quiet, friendship is produced from strife, the fire of anger being extinguished; and you yourself will not appear to be destitute of reason.

Symbol 10

The preceding symbol is corroborated by the next, *turn away from yourself every sharp edge.* For to whomsoever it shall be turned, he will be injured. And this counsels us to use prudence, and not to indulge in anger; for that sharp part or edge of the mind, which we call anger, is void of reason and wisdom: for anger boils like a pot upon the fire, converting the mind to nothing but its own emotions, and breaking up the judgment. One therefore should establish his soul in tranquility by protecting and restraining it from anger, as one does not make brass sound without touching it. This passion therefore must be suppressed by reason.

Symbol 11

This, *help a man to take up a burden, but not to lay it down,* exhorts us to fortitude. For whoever takes up a burden, signifies that he undertakes an action of labor and energy; but he who lays one down, of rest and remission. So that the symbol has this meaning: do not become either to yourself or another the cause of an indolent and effeminate mode of conduct; for every useful thing is acquired by labor. This symbol the Pythagoreans called Herculean, it being confirmed as it were by his labors. For during his association with men, he often returned from great and terrible dangers, indignantly rejecting indolence. For rectitude of conduct is produced from acting and working, but not from sluggishness.

Symbol 12

Put the shoe on the right foot first, but put the left foot first in the bath tub, exhorts to practical wisdom. For the symbol advises us to place honest actions about us as right handed; but to reject and throw away the bad as being left-handed.

Symbol 13

This, *speak not about Pythagoric concerns without light,* specially exhorts to the acquisition of intellectual prudence. For this is similar to the light of the soul, to which being definite it gives bounds, and leads as it were from darkness into light. It is right, therefore, to place intellect as a leader of everything beautiful in life, but especially in Pythagoric dogmas, for these cannot be known without light.

Symbol 14

This, *do not step above the beam of the balance,* exhorts us to the exercise of justice, to the honoring equality and moderation above all things, and to the knowledge of justice as the most perfect virtue, to which the other virtues give completion, and without which none of the other virtues are of any advantage. It also counsels us, that it is right to know this virtue not superficially but through theorems and scientific demonstrations. But this knowledge is the work of no other art and science than the Pythagoric philosophy alone, which in a transcendent degree honors disciplines before everything else.

Symbol 15

To the same end as the preceding contributes the next symbol, *traveling from home, turn not back, for the Furies will go back with you.* For this exhorts to Philosophy and a self-acting energy according to intellect—and, further, this symbol clearly shows and teaches, that the one studying philosophy must separate himself from all corporeal and sensible things, and truly meditate upon death, proceeding without turning back to intelligible and incorporeal essences, which are always the same in every respect, through appropriate disciplines. For traveling is a change of place, but death is the separation of the soul from the body; and this is attained if we truly philosophize without the aid of the sensible and corporeal activities, but use the pure intellect to reach the apprehension of the truth in things that really exist, which is acknowledged to be wisdom. But having undertaken the study of Philosophy do not abandon it, nor be drawn back to the former and corporeal things in which you were nurtured. For a return to the vulgar plane will produce great repentance, the darkness of corporeal things constituting a serious impediment to genuine apprehensions of things. And repentance is called an Erinnys or a Fury.

Symbol 16

This, *do not urinate facing the sun,* advises that we do nothing bestial—but, contemplating Heaven and the Sun, philosophize, the light of truth showing you the way; and remember that while studying Philosophy nothing base or vulgar should rule or contaminate the mind, but ascent to the Gods and wisdom through the contemplation of celestial things. And having applied to the study of Philosophy, and purifying yourself by the light of truth which is in it, and concentrating yourself on this study, acquire a knowledge of Theology, Physiology, Astronomy, and the Science of causes, which surpasses all the rest—but do nothing which is bestial or irrational.

Symbol 17

To the same end as the preceding is this, *clean not a seat with a torch.* For not only because a torch is of a purifying nature, in consequence of its rapid and abundant participation in fire, like sulphur, and is said to be as it were divine, does this symbol exhort us not to defile it, since it is itself of a nature which removes all sordid or defiling things, nor to oppose its natural quality by defiling that which is an impediment to defilement—but much more, lest we should mingle the characteristics of wisdom with those things which are peculiar to the animal nature. For a torch, by virtue of its brightness, is compared to Philosophy; but a seat, by reason of its lowness, to animality.

Symbol 18

This, *nourish a cock, but do not sacrifice it; for it is sacred to the sun and the moon,* advises us to nourish and not neglect those things which perish and are destroyed because they are mighty proofs of the union, connection, sympathy, and consent of the world. So it exhorts us to apprehend the theory and philosophy of the universe. For though the truth concerning the universe is naturally recondite, and sufficiently difficult of investigation, it must nevertheless be sought and investigated by man, and chiefly through Philosophy. For it is truly impossible to discover it through any other study or pursuit. But philosophy receiving certain sparks from nature blows them up into a great flame, making them more active through the disciplines or sciences which she possesses. Wherefore we should philosophize.

Symbol 19

This, *do not sit upon a choenix [bushel],* one may show to be specially of a Pythagoric character, from what has been previously said. For since nutriment is to be measured by the corporeal and animal nature and not by a bushel, do not remain intellectually indolent, nor uninitiated into Philosophy; but, devoting yourself to philosophic study, give great care and attention to the diviner part of yourself, which is the soul, and much greater care to the highest part of the soul, which is the intellect, the nutriment of which is not measured by a bushel but by contemplation and discipline.

Symbol 20

This, *rear nothing which has crooked nails,* advises something which is still more Pythagorical. Be beneficent and communicative, and endeavor to make others such also, accustoming yourself to give and receive without grudging or envy; nor take all things insatiably, not giving anything. For the animals which have crooked nails are naturally so constituted that they receive and snatch quickly and readily, but do not easily let go, or impart to others, by reason of the tenacity of their nails because they are crooked: just as hooks are so made that they quickly seize a thing, but will hardly release it unless they are pushed forward and thereby freed. But since nature has given us hands, in order that we may give and receive according to the precept, and straight instead of crooked fingers, therefore we should not imitate those animals which have crooked nails, being made by the creator in a different manner from us, but rather mutually to communicate to and receive from one another, being incited to do this by those who first gave names to things, who called the right hand more excellent than the left, not only because it receives but also because it is able to impart. Wherefore we should act justly, and for that reason philosophize: for justice is a certain return or retribution and remuneration, equalizing the abounding and deficient by reciprocal gifts.

Symbol 21

This, *cut not in the way,* shows that truth is one, but falsehood many. This is evidenced by the fact that the nature ["quiddity"] of everything is expressed in only one way, if we speak rightly, but what it is not is expressed in innumerable ways. But the "way" seems to signify Philosophy. This symbol therefore says: choose that philosophy and that way to Philosophy in which there is no division, and in which you will not dogmatize contrary doctrines, but pursue those which are stable and established by scientific demonstration through mathematical disciplines and contemplation—which is the same as to say, philosophize Pythagorically. And this indeed is possible. But the [so-called] philosophy which is based on corporeal and sensuous things, which the youthful and immature in mind use insatiably, and which teaches that God and qualities and the soul and virtues and, in brief, all the primary causes of things, are of a corporeal nature, is weak and easily refuted, as is shown by the different refutations of those who have noticed it. On the contrary, the philosophy which is based on and works through incorporeal, intelligible, immaterial and perpetual essences, which are ever the same in themselves and in relation to each other, and never receive corruption or change, this philosophy, similar to the essences with which it deals, is infallible and stable, and effective of firm and irrefragable demonstration. This precept therefore counsels us, when we philosophize and proceed in the way pointed out, to avoid the reception of corporeal and multiple and visible things, but to intimately apply ourselves to the essence of incorporeal natures, which are never dissimilar to themselves, by reason of the truth and infallibility which they naturally have.

Symbol 22

This, *do not receive a swallow into your house,* advises that you do not admit to your dogmas one who is indolent, who does not labor constantly, and who is not a firm adherent of the Pythagorean sect, and endued with intelligence; for these require the most zealous attention and great intellectual toil on account of the variety and abstruseness of the several disciplines. The symbol uses the swallow as an image of indolence and lack of perseverance, because this bird comes to us only in one season of the year and stays with us but a short time; but for the most of the year is absent and out of our sight.

Symbol 23

From this, *do not wear a ring,* agreeably to the Pythagoric doctrine, there is the following exhortation: a ring like a chain encircles the finger of the wearer, but with this difference, that it pinches not nor pains, but fits as easily as if it naturally belonged to that part; and the body is a chain or bond of this kind to the soul. *Do not wear a ring,* therefore, signifies, *philosophize truly, and separate your soul from the bond which surrounds it.* For a contemplation of death and separation of the soul from the body is philosophy. Cultivate therefore with great earnestness the Pythagorean philosophy which separates the soul through intellect from all corporeal things, and busies itself about intelligible and immaterial essences by means of theoretic disciplines. But exterminate your sins and all things which hold you back and impede philosophizing, namely occupations and diversions of the body, excessive eating and unseasonable repletions, which fetter the body and continually breed diseases and molestations.

Symbol 24

This, *inscribe not the image of God in a ring,* agreeably to the foregoing conception, contains the following exhortation: Philosophize, and above all things consider the Gods as having an incorporeal essence. For this is the most principal root and foundation of the Pythagoric dogmas, on which nearly all of them are based, and by which they are strengthened even to the end. Do not therefore think that the Gods use forms which are corporeal, nor that they are contained by a material subject, and bound as it were by a chain to a material body, like animals. But the engravings in rings exhibit the bond which subsists through the ring, its corporeal nature and sensible form, and the view as it were of one of the several animals which becomes apparent through the engraving, from which we should specially separate the genus of the Gods, as being intelligible and eternal, and always subsisting according to the same end in a similar manner, as we have particularly, most fully, and scientifically shown in our treatise *Concerning the Gods.*[31]

Symbol 25

This, *look not in a glass by lamp-light,* counsels us more Pythagorically to philosophize—not pursuing the phantasies of sense, which produce indeed a kind of light about our apprehensions of things similar to that of a lamp, but which is neither natural nor true, but cultivating the scientific conceptions according to intellect by which a bright and unfailing light is produced in and about the eye of the soul, which flows from all intellections and intelligibles and the contemplation of these, but not from corporeal and sensuous things: for these are in a continuous fluxion and mutation, as has often been shown, and are in no respect stable or existing similar to themselves, whereby they might sustain a firm and scientific apprehension and knowledge, like the others.

31) This work is unfortunately lost.

Symbol 26

This, *do not indulge in immoderate laughter,* shows that we should conquer and rule the passions by philosophic reason, and that we should restrain the mutable and unstable parts of human nature. Follow therefore the dictates of right reason; be neither elated by good fortune, nor dejected by bad, not admitting that any change worthy of attention takes place in either of these. The symbol names laughter above all other affections, because it alone is most clearly apparent, subsisting like a certain efflorescence and inflammation of the disposition proceeding as far as to the countenance. Perhaps, also, since laughter is peculiar to man only of all animals, whence some define a man to be an animal capable of laughing, it is evidenced by this precept that we should not firmly and immutably remain in the human condition merely, but to the extent of our power should become similar to the Deity, by philosophizing and by abandoning the characteristic habits and actions of men, and should prefer the rational, by which we are differentiated from other animals, to the visible.

Symbol 27

This, *do not cut your nails while sacrificing,* is exhortative to friendship. For of our relations and those allied to us by blood the nearest to us are brothers, children, and parents; who are similar to those parts of our body which cannot be taken away without pain and mutilation, such as fingers, hands, ears, noses and the like: but others who are more distantly related to us, such as the children of cousins, or of uncles, or of those related to us by marriage—these are similar to those parts of our body which may be cut off without pain, such as hair, nails and the like. Wishing therefore to refer to those relations whom on account of their remoteness we neglect at times, the symbol uses the word "nails" and says: do not cast away these entirely [do not ignore them altogether] but, while sacrificing, even though neglected by you at other times, take them with you and renew your familiarity with them.

Symbol 28

This, *do not readily seize everyone with your right hand,* declares: extend not your right hand easily, that is, do not draw to yourself nor attempt to elevate to the Pythagorean association by extending the right hand to them, those who are unfit and uninitiated. Moreover, to those who have not been long tested by disciplines and doctrines, and are not proved worthy to participate in temperance, and of the five year silence and other probationary trials, the right hand ought not to be given.

Symbol 29

This, *when you rise from bed disorder the covering, and efface the impression of the body,* counsels that, studying and practicing philosophy, you should become familiar with intelligible and incorporeal essences: therefore, as soon as you rise from the sleep of ignorance and intellectual darkness, which is similar to that of the night, draw up with yourself nothing corporeal to the light of Philosophy, which is similar to that of day, but efface from your memory all traces of that sleep of ignorance.

Symbol 30

This, *eat not the heart,* signifies that it is not right to sunder the union and cohesion of the universe. Moreover, it advises: be not envious, but philanthropic, and communicative. Hence it exhorts to the study of Philosophy. For Philosophy alone of all the sciences and arts envies not the goods of others, nor rejoices in the evils of neighbors; but declares that all men are by nature allied to each other, subject to the like passions, exposed to one common fortune, and alike ignorant of the future. Wherefore this symbol exhorts us to sympathy and mutual love, and to be truly communicative, since we are rational animals.

Symbol 31

This, *eat not the brain,* is similar to the preceding, for the brain is the principal instrument of intellectual action. The symbol therefore obscurely signifies that we ought not to despise or distort things and dogmas which have been the objects of judicious investigation. But these will be such as have been investigated and considered by intellect and the principal instruments of intellectual apprehension, becoming equal to those comprehended by science. For things of this kind are to be surveyed not through and by the instruments of the irrational form of the soul, namely the heart and the liver, but through the pure rational nature: hence to oppose these is folly. But the symbol rather exhorts us to venerate the fountain of intelligence, and the most proximate instrument of intellectual perception, through which we may acquire contemplation, science, and the universal wisdom, and by which we may truly philosophize, and neither to confound nor obscure the vestiges of it.

Symbol 32

This, *spit upon the cuttings of your hair and the parings of your nails,* declares that those things are easily despised which are born with you but are practically inanimate, just as those things are more honored which participate more of soul: therefore, when you have applied yourself to Philosophy honor those things which are demonstrated through the soul and intellect, without the organs of sense, and through theoretic science, but despise and spit upon those things which are perceived without the intelligible light, through the organs of the senses which are born with us and which lack the capacity to reach the permanency of the intellect.

Symbol 33

This, *do not receive the fish Erythrinus,* seems to refer merely to the etymology of the word. For it signifies: receive not an unblushing and impudent man; nor, on the contrary, one who is stupidly astonished and who blushes at everything, and is humble in the extreme, through the imbecility of his intellect and reasoning power. Hence this also is understood: Be not yourself such a one.

Symbol 34

This, *destroy the print of a pot in the ashes,* signifies that he who applies himself to the study of Philosophy must forget the confusion and grossness which are peculiar to corporeal and sensible demonstrations, and use altogether demonstrations through intelligible essences. "Ashes" here means or represents the dust or sand in a mathematical table, in which the demonstrations and figures are drawn.

Symbol 35

This, *draw not near to that which has gold, in order to produce children,* does not refer to a woman, but to that sect and philosophy which has much of the corporeal in it, and a gravitating tendency downwards. For gold is the heaviest of all things in the earth, and most likely to move toward the center, which is the peculiarity of corporeal weight. But the phrase *draw near* not only signifies to be connected with, but also to approach toward, and to be seated near, another.

Symbol 36

This, *honor more a figure and step than a figure and three obols,* advises to philosophize, and cultivate mathematical disciplines, not superficially but thoroughly, and by them, as if they were steps of a ladder, to ascend to the proposed end; but to despise those things which are honored and considered of great value by the multitude; and to reverence above all the Italic philosophy, which speculates upon incorporeal essences in themselves, in preference to the Ionic, which chiefly investigates bodies.

Symbol 37

This, *abstain from beans,* advises us to beware of everything which is corruptive of our converse with the Gods and divine prophecy.

Symbol 38

This, *transplant mallows in your garden, but eat them not,* obscurely signifies that plants of this kind turn with the sun, and directs that this should be noticed by us. The symbol also adds, *transplant,* that is to say, observe its nature, its tendency toward, and sympathy with, the sun; but rest not satisfied, nor dwell upon this, but transfer, and as it were transplant, your conception to kindred plants and herbs, and also to animals which are not kindred, to stones and rivers, and in brief, to natures of every kind.

For you will find them to be prolific and multiform, and admirably abundant; and this to one who begins from the mallows, as from a root and principle, is significant of the union and cohesion of the cosmos. Not only, therefore, do not destroy or obliterate observations of this kind, but increase and multiply them as it were by transplantation.

Symbol 39

This, *abstain from the use of living creatures,* exhorts to justice, with a due regard for what is of a kindred nature, and a sympathetic treatment of life which is similar to our own.

Through all the foregoing explanations, therefore, appears the mode of exhortation through symbols containing much of the ancient and Pythagoric method. But since we have expounded all modes of exhortation, we will here conclude our treatise on the subject.

THE GOLDEN VERSES OF PYTHAGORAS

The famous Golden Verses attributed to Pythagoras may not have originated with him, as the majority of critics assert, but they contain an epitome of his philosophy, enunciating his chief precepts in a harmonious, elegant and concise form. If these precepts were put into practice the result would be a moral and intellectual revolution in human life, which would be of an inestimable benefit to mankind. The Golden Verses have been often edited, and translated into many languages. An excellent English version by the Rev. John Norris, a Platonic thinker of high reputation, author of a curious and abstruse "Essay on the Intelligible World," of great value, was published in 1682, and is reprinted for the sake of those who desire to read the complete text of the Verses. Hierocles' *Commentary* is one of the finest ethical treatises ever written, and richly deserves a continuous, profound study.

First the Immortal Gods as ranked by law
Honour, and use an oath with holy awe.
Then honour Heroes which Mankind excell,
And Dæmons of the earth, by living well.
Your parents next and those of nearest blood,
Then other Friends regard as they are good.
Yield to mild words and offices of love,
Doe not for little faults your friend remove.
This is no more than what in you doth lye,
For power dwells hard by necessity.
Doe these things so; but those restrain you must
Your Appetite, your Sleep, your Anger and Lust.
From filthy actions at all times forbear,
Whether with others or alone you are;
And of all things yourself learn to revere.
In Deed and Word to Justice have an eye;
Doe not the lest thing unadvisedly.
But know that all must to the shades below,
That riches sometimes ebb and sometimes flow.

Bear patiently what ill by Heaven is sent,
Add not unto your griefs by discontent.
Yet rid them if you can, but know withall,
Few of those Thunder storms on good men fall.
Oft good and ill doe in discourse unite,
Be not too apt to admire, nor yet to slight.
But if through errour any speak amiss,
Endure it with mildness, but be sure of this,
That none by word or action you entice
To doe or speak to your own prejudice.
Think before action Folly to prevent;
Rash words and acts are their own punishment.
That doe, which done, after you'll ne'er repent.
That which you know not, doe not undertake,
But learn what's fit, if life you'll pleasant make.
Health is a thing you ought not to despise,
In Diet use a mean, and exercise;
And that's a mean whence does no damage rise.
Be neat, but not luxurious in your fare,
How you incur men's censure have a care.
Let not thy state in ill timed treats be spent,
Like one that knows not what's magnificent,
Nor by a thrift untimely rake too clean,
'Tis best in every thing to use a mean.
Be not mischievous to yourself; advise
Before you act, and never let your eyes
The sweet refreshings of soft slumber taste,
Till you have thrice severe reflections past,
On th' actions of the day from first to last.
Wherein have I transgressed? What done have I?
What duty unperformed have I passed by?
And if your actions ill on search you find,
Let Grief; if good, let joy, possess your mind.
This doe, this think, to this your heart incline,
This way will lead you to the life Divine.
Believ't, I swear by him who did us show
The mystery of FOUR, whence all things flow,

Then to your work, having prayed Heaven to send,
On what you undertake, a happy end.
This Course, if you observe, you shall know then
The constitution both of Gods and men.
The due extent of all things you shall see,
And Nature in her Uniformitie.
That so your ignorance may not suggest
Vain hopes of what you cannot be possest.
You'll see how poor, unfortunate mankind
To hurt themselves are studiously inclined,
To all approaching good, both deaf and blind.
The way to cure their ills is known to few,
Such a besotting fate do men pursue.
They're on cylinders still roll'd up and down,
And with full tides of evil overflown,
A cursed inbred strife doth work within,
The cause of all this misery and sin,
Which must not be provoked to open field,
The way to conquer here's to fly and yield.
And now from ill, Great Father, set us free,
Or teach us all to know ourselves and Thee.
Courage, my soul; Great Jove is their allie,
Their duty who by Nature's light descry;
These Rules if to that number you retain,
You'll keep, and purge your Soul from every stain.
Abstain from meats which you forbidden find
In our Traditions, wherein are defined
The Purgings and Solution of the Mind.
Consider this: then in the highest sphere
Enthrone your Reason, the best Charioteer.
So when unbodyed you shall freely rove
In the unbounded Regions above,
You an immortal God shall then commence,
Advanced beyond Mortality and Sense.

FRAGMENTS OF IAMBLICHUS

FROM THE EPISTLE TO MACEDONIOS CONCERNING FATE[1]

I. All beings owe their existence to the One, for even the first being itself is derived directly from the One. Much more do universal causes owe their power or efficiency to the One, and are held together in one connecting chain, and are moved in harmony, by the [Supreme] Principle which is prior to the many. According to this theory, since natural causes are multiform and manifold, and depend on many principles, and from one universal cause multitude is suspended, and all things are interwoven with each other by and through one bond, the bond or chain of many causes is referred to the one power most comprehensive of cause, which is the bond of many causes. Therefore this one is the bond constituted from the multitude: nor does it make the supervening union from the connection, nor is it dispersed among particulars or individuals, but according to a guiding and predetermined chain of causes in itself, it perfects all things, binds them in itself, and leads them uniformly to itself. Wherefore Fate or Destiny may be defined as one supreme order containing all other orders together in itself.

II. The essence of the soul is immaterial, independent, incorporeal, totally ungenerated and indestructible, having from itself existence and life, wholly self-motive, and the principle of nature and all motions. Being of such a character, therefore, it comprehends in itself a life free from and independent of the body. So far, therefore, as it gives itself to the things of generation, and subjects itself to the revolution of the universe, so far it is controlled by Fate, and becomes subservient to the physical necessities; but so far as it exercises its intellectual energy independently, so far it voluntarily acts in regard to its own affairs, and apprehends the divine and good and intelligible.

III. Wherefore it behooves us to live the life of the intellect and of

---

1) Stobæus: *Eclog. Phys.* Lib. I, cap. 6, Lib. II, cap. 8.

the Gods, since this alone gives unfettered power to the soul, and liberates us from the bonds of necessity; and causes us to live not merely a human but a divine life, and one naturally full of divine goods.

IV. And, to speak briefly, the motions produced in and about the world by Fate are similar to the immaterial and intellectual activities and motions in the intelligible world, and the order of Fate is an image of the intelligible and undefiled order. But secondary causes are referred to prior causes, and the multitude in generation to the indivisible essence or nature; and thus all the things of Fate are conjoined with the pre-guiding Providence. By the same essence, therefore, Fate is interwoven with Providence, and by virtue of its nature Providence is also Fate, and subsists from and about it. These things being so, the principle of human actions is in harmony with both these principles, namely Providence and Fate, of the universe; but there is also in us a principle of actions, i.e. the rational soul, which is independent of nature and not subject to the motion of the universe. On account of this it is not contained in the motion of the universe: because the soul follows its own motion and not the motion of the universe, it is above Fate; and because the universe does not influence it, it is of a superior order, but so far as it is distributed to all the parts of the universe and is allotted certain divisions from all the elements, and is used by all these, the soul is contained in the order of Fate and acts in connection with it, fills it, and uses it rightly. And so far as the soul contains in herself a pure reason and the perfect, and is independent and self-motive, acting from herself, so far she is liberated from all external things. But so far as she assumes other lives, falling into generation and associating with the body, so far she is interwoven with the order of the universe.

V. But if anyone thinks that by introducing chance and fortune he will destroy order, let him learn that there is nothing in the universe unordered or incoherent, nor without cause, nor indeterminate, nor without a purpose, nor any thing proceeding from nothing, and arising by accident. Therefore the order and series of causes is not destroyed by chance, nor the union of principles, nor the mastery of rule of the primary principles extending through and over all things. It is better therefore to define Fortune as the order of superior things, and of other things which are inferior, so far as she is an overseer of events and a concomitant cause for them, and anterior to them; thus Fortune we at one time call a god, and at another a dæmon. For when there are superior causes of events a god is the principle or ruler of them; but when there are natural causes, a dæmon. Therefore all things perpetually become from causes, nor is anything introduced into generation without order.

VI. Why are the goods of life apparently distributed contrary to desert or undeservedly? But this question it is not right to ask, since on nothing else than man himself and on the will of man do true goods depend: and the chief of these are determined by the will. But the question originates in the ignorance of the multitude. There is no fruit of virtue other than itself. The upright or virtuous man is not injured by fortune, for the magnitude of his soul makes him superior to any event or accident. Neither do evils happen to him contrary to nature, since the excellence and perfection of the soul satisfy the highest principle of man. And, indeed, the things which seem to be evil or adverse exercise, secure and augment virtue; and without them it is impossible for men to become good and upright. And therefore it is the essential characteristic of the upright man to honor virtue above all other things, and to place the perfection of reason in a happy life alone: other things he holds as nothing, and despises them. Since therefore the soul constitutes the real man, and the soul is intellectual and immortal, and its virtue, good, and end subsist in the divine life, truly nothing of mortal things can either augment the perfect life or diminish its felicity. In brief, our felicity consists in the intellectual life, so nothing of intermediary things can either increase or subvert it. In vain therefore are fortune and its worthless gifts praised by men.

FROM THE EPISTLE CONCERNING TEMPERANCE[2]

I. Every virtue despises everything of a mortal form or nature, but chiefly honors the immortal. But this is especially the serious purpose of Temperance, holding in contempt the pleasures which

2) Stobæus: *Flor*. Lib. IV. 61, etc., Lib. V. 136.

nail the soul to the body, and firmly established on holy pedestals, as Plato says.[3]

II. For how does Temperance not make us perfect, banishing wholly from us the imperfect and affective? You may know that this is the case by considering, for example, the story of Bellerophon, how, aided by Temperance, he destroyed the Chimæra, and every brutal, savage, and wild race. In brief, the excessive domination of the affections does not permit men to be men, but draws them down to the irrational nature, and the brutal and the lawless.

III. But excellent order or rightness of conduct restraining the pleasures within proportionate bounds preserves both families and cities, according to the saying of Crates. Moreover, it brings us near in a certain respect to the form of the Gods. Wherefore Perseus, advancing to the highest good of Temperance, guided by Athena, cut off the head of the Gorgon, which signifies, I think, Desire drawing men down into matter, and petrifying them by a stupifying abundance of material experiences.

IV. The foundation, therefore, of Virtue, as Socrates said, is the mastery of sensual pleasures; and Temperance is viewed as the ornament of all goods, as Plato affirmed. But this Virtue is the stability of the best habits, in my opinion.

V. Hence I affirm with absolute confidence, what is really acknowledged, that the beauty of Temperance extends through all the virtues, and unites all the virtues in one harmony, infusing in them due proportion and union with each other. Temperance [sophrosyne] being therefore of such a character supplies assistance to the implanting of the other virtues; and when they are implanted gives to them a perpetual security.

VI. The constitution of the seasons of the year and the blending of the elements with each other preserve a harmony or accord most beautiful and temperate. And all this, on account of the character or order of the most beautiful proportions, is called the cosmos or universe.

VII. I affirm therefore the same things about all the powers of the soul, namely the symmetry or due proportion which they have to

3) Plato, *Phædrus*, 254B.

each other, the arrangement of spirit, desire, and reason, according to the rank appropriate to each. And as to these, if the division of that which rules and is ruled is seasonably or rightly made in that which is fitting, sophrosyne will be multiform.

FROM THE EPISTLE TO ASPHALIOS ON WISDOM[4]

The argument shows that Wisdom, being the leader of the virtues, and using all of them—just as the intellectual eye perceives by the intellectual light the objects which are present to it—assigns to them their orders and measures and most appropriate disposition. Wisdom, then, as a primary subsistence receives its origin from a pure and perfect intellect. Hence it looks to the same intellect, is perfected by it, and has this as the measure and most beautiful exemplar of all its activities. If also there is to us a certain communion with the Gods, it is specially constituted through this virtue; and through this we are assimilated to them in the highest degree. And the knowledge, too, of such things as are good, profitable and beautiful, and of the contraries to these, comes to us from this virtue; and the judgment and correction of works which ought to be done are by this directed. And, to speak summarily, Wisdom is a certain executive leader of men and of the whole order of nature; and referring cities and homes and the life of everyone to a divine exemplar, it forms them according to the best similitude— exterminating some things, and purifying others. Thus, therefore, Wisdom renders its possessors similar to Divinity.

FROM THE EPISTLE TO SOPATER ON TRUTH[5]

Truth, as the name implies, makes a conversion toward the Gods and their undefiled actuality; but opinionative (doxastic) imitation which, as Plato says, is fabricative of images, wanders about that which is atheistic and dark. And the former indeed received its perfection in intelligible and divine forms, and real beings which are always the same; but the latter looks to that which is formless, and non-being, and which has a mutable subsistence, and for this

---

4) Stobæus: *Flor*. Lib. III. 55.
5) Stobæus: *Flor*. Lib. X. 14.

reason its power to see is blunted. The former contemplates that which is; but the latter apprehends such a form as appears to the many. Hence truth associates with intellect, and increases our intellectual nature; but doxastic imitation, looking to that which always seems to be, hunts after folly and deceives.

[Plato considers truth multifariously. According to his doctrine the highest truth is characterized by unity, and is the light proceeding from *the good,* which imparts *purity* and *union* to intelligibles. The truth which is next in dignity is that which proceeds from intelligibles, and illuminates the intellectual orders, and which an essence unfigured, uncolored and intangible first receives, where also the plain of truth is located, as it is written in the *Phædrus.* The third kind of truth is that which is connascent with souls, and which through intelligence comes into contact with true being. For the psychical light is the third from the intelligible, the intellectual deriving its plenitude from the intelligible light, and the psychical from the intellectual. And the last kind of truth is that which is in sensibles, which is full of error and inaccuracy through sense, and the instability of its object. For a material nature is perpetually flowing, and is not naturally adapted to abide even for a moment.— Thomas Taylor.]

EXCERPTS FROM THE COMMENTARY OF PROCLUS ON THE CHALDEAN ORACLES[1]

I. The eternal orders are the temples and habitations of the Gods, and the paternal order is the all-receptive temple of the Father which receives and unites ascending souls. The angelic order in a characteristic way leads souls upward to the celestial region, "appearing about the soul," according to the Oracle, i.e., illuminating it thoroughly, and causing it to be full of undefiled fire, which imparts to it an immutable and tranquil order and power, through or by which it is not rushed into material disorder, but is united with the light of divine things: this, further, retains it in its native place, and causes it to be unmixed with matter, elevating the spirit by heat and raising it on high by means of the anagogic life. For the heating of the spirit is the imparting of life. But it is wholly elevated by hastening into the celestial region, just as by gravitating downward it is carried into matter or the region of generation. But the end of ascents is the participation in divine fruits and the filling the soul with divine fire, which is the contemplation of God, the soul being placed in the presence of the Father.

The soul celebrating divine things is perfected, according to the Oracle, placing before and carrying to the Father the ineffable symbols of the Father, which the Father placed in the soul in the first progression of essence. For such are the intellectual and invisible hymns of the ascending soul, awakening the memory of harmonic reasons, which bear the inexpressible images in it of the divine powers.

II. [The immortal depth of the soul should be the leader, but

---

1) *Eclogæ e Proclo De Philosophia Chaldaica nunc primum edidit et commentatus est Albert Jahnius . . . Hal.* 1891. These are precious fragments of a copious treatise on the Chaldaic Oracles, those wondrous remnants of ancient wisdom, by Proclus, one of the "most refulgent links" in the Golden Chain of Platonic Succession. The loss of this and other profound works of Proclus has deprived the students of divine Philosophy of much knowledge of the highest species and greatest value.

vehemently extend all your eyes upwards.—*Chaldean Oracles*]

The Oracle says that the depth of the soul is its triadic gnostic powers, namely intelligible, discursive, and doxastic or opinionative, but that all the eyes are its triadic gnostic activities. For the eye is the symbol of knowledge, but life of desire: and each of these is a triad. But the earth, from which it is necessary that the heart be raised, signifies all material and mutable things in generation, i.e. the terrestrial life and every corporeal form. To which follows, the Oracle adds, the contemplation of the paternal monad, the pure joy in reference to this contemplation, and a steady tranquility from this intelligible survey.

From these it is evident that the good of this contemplation is mixed from the apprehension and the joy which naturally accompanies it. For every life having an energy which is by its nature easily and quickly liberated is allotted a connate or coordinate pleasure. The hymn of the Father does not consist of compound discourses nor the preparation of sacred rites. For being alone incorruptible he does not receive a corruptible hymn. Let us not therefore imagine that we may persuade the Master of true discourses by a strange hurricane of words, nor by show or parade adorned with artificial rites: for God loves the simple, unadorned beauty of form. Let us therefore consecrate this hymn to God as an assimilation to or becoming like him: let us leave this earthly sphere, which is of a transient nature: let us come to the true end: let us know the Master: let us love the Father: let us obey the one calling: let us run to the hot, flying from the cold. Let us become fire: let us travel through fire. We have a quick and easy way to the ascent to the Father. The Father will guide, pointing out the ways of fire: let us not flow with the humble stream of Lethe, the river of oblivion.

III. The body is the root of evil, just as the Intellect is the root of Virtue. For Virtue blossoms for souls in the celestial region, but evil comes to souls from the worse, in the region of matter. The casting into the material region the evil which is eliminated from our nature will enable the soul to go wherever it may aspire. It is now temporarily allotted to the whole of generation or the material nature, since evils are here and of necessity revolve in and around this place. And our body is a part of generation or the sphere of time and sense, but another part, namely the soul, is able to act unsubdued by the power of generation, but cannot conquer the whole of generation, unless we destroy the being or essence of it.

Into the material sphere, therefore, we must cast jealousy and envy, whence the soul drew them. For material things have matter as a nurse. And "the not extinguishing" or restraining the tendency of the mind to the worse does not refer to a mere temporary disappearance of it, just as all the affections which are restrained in a certain being are contained in it and fill it with their own heat. But instead of restraining, cast it out, not keeping within you that which is only dammed up. On account of which the Oracle adds: "Do not defile the spirit through that which is within and hidden." But envy is material: for it dwells with the privation of goods. And privation co-exists with unproductive matter. But the theurgic race is beneficent, and devoted to a zealous imitation of the goodness of God, but it is not drawn down to the contentiousness and enmity of men. But these affections are enclosed in souls, imparting to the spirit a certain material character, and filling it with material privation and lifelessness.

IV. The soul consisting according to its discursive reason knows or cognizes true or divine beings. But establishing itself in the intellectual life of its peculiar essence, it knows all things by simple and impartible intuitions. Ascending to the One, and folding up and laying aside all multitude which is in itself, it actualizes itself enthusiastically and is united to the super-intellectual summit. For everywhere the similar is naturally united to the similar, and every cognition through similitude binds to that which is known the knower: to the sensible or object of sense-perception the perceptive cognition, to cognizable objects discursive reason, to intelligible objects intelligible cognition, and therefore also to that which is prior to intellect the flower of the intellect is correspondent. For as in other things not intellect, but the cause superior to intellect is highest, so in souls the first form of energy is not intellectual but that which is more divine than the intellect. And every soul and every intellect have twofold activities, the unical activities which are better than intellection, and the intelligible activities. It is necessary therefore to apprehend this intelligible, which exists *per se,* and the summit of existence, our eyes being closed to all other lives and powers. For as we apprehend intellect by becoming intellectual form, so becoming uniform we ascend to union, standing on the characteristic summit of intellect—since even the eye does not otherwise see the sun than by becoming solar-formed, but not by the light from fire.

Moreover, it is plain that this intelligible cannot be apprehended by a reasoning process. But, as the Oracle says, if you apply your intellect, you will come by intellectual intuitions into contact with this intelligible, and thus you will apprehend it as understanding some particular things, i.e. you cannot grasp this intelligible by laying hold of it according to a certain measure of form and knowledge. For however simple such intellections may be, they are deprived of the unific simplicity of the intelligible, and are carried into secondary conditions of the intellect, proceeding into a multitude of intelligible things. For no object of knowledge is known through or by an inferior knowledge: neither therefore is that which is above intellect known through intellect. For all at once the intellect hurls or projects itself to a certain thing, and pronounces that this or that is apprehended, which dictum is the second from the intelligible. But if by the flower of our intellect we apprehend this intelligible, established on the summit of the first intelligible triad, are we united by a certain relation to the One which is uncoordinated with all things, and imparticipable? For if the first Father is said by the Oracle to hastily withdraw himself from Intellect and Power, what is that which lacks nothing that it should thus be withdrawn, but is withdrawn or isolated from all things simply, and is celebrated as the God of all? Is this not also said by the Oracle in another place about the Primary Father? And as for the first power of the sacred reason: what is that which is above this, and does not participate in this, and is said by the Oracle to be sacred? And if the reason shining forth is named by the Oracle as a more ineffable reason, it is necessary that prior to reason Silence should subsist as a reason or productive principle, and prior to every sacred reason the deifying cause.

As therefore beyond the intelligibles are the reasons or productive principles of intelligibles, things being united, so the productive principle in them subsists from another more ineffable unity, though there is a reason of the Silence prior to intelligibles, but a Silence of silent intelligibles. Perhaps, therefore, this flower of the intellect is not the flower of our whole soul. But this, i.e., the flower of the intellect, is the most unific of our intellectual life, and the flower of the soul is the one of all the psychical powers, they being multiform. For we are not intellect alone, but discursive reason and opinion and attention and will, and prior to these powers we are one essence and many, partible and impartible. And the one shining forth is twofold: one or the flower of the soul being the first of our powers, the other being the whole essence of the center and of all the all-various powers about it; but this, i.e. the flower of the soul, alone unites us to the Father of the intelligibles. For the one is intellectual, but this is apprehended by the Paternal Intellect according to the unity (*henad*) which is in it. But the unity (*henad*) to which all the psychical powers verge and in which they unite and center alone naturally leads us to the Principle which is beyond all beings, and is the unifying power of all that is in us. So that we are rooted or planted essentially in this Principle, and by being rooted, even though we may descend from the intelligible region, we will not be estranged from our cause.

V. Philosophy says that a forgetfulness of eternal reasons is the cause of the departure of the soul from the Gods, and that a reminiscence of the knowledge of the eternal reasons or Ideas is the cause of the return to them, but the Oracles assert that the forgetfulness and reminiscence of the paternal symbols are respectively the causes of the departure and return. Both statements are in harmony. For the soul is constituted from intellectual reasons and divine symbols, of which the former proceed from the intellectual species, but the latter from the divine unities: and we are images of the intellectual essences, but statues of the unknown symbols. And just as every soul is a fullness (*pleroma*) of forms, but subsists wholly or simply according to one cause, thus also it indeed participates in all symbols, through which it is united to divine things, but the summit of the soul in the one is separated or divided, so that every multitude in the soul is led into one summit. For it is necessary to know that every soul differs from every other soul according to form or specifically, and that there are as many souls as there are species of souls. For there is first indeed according to one form a hypostasis of many individual, unific forms about matter and the composites of beings, there being one subject nature participating variously in the same form: then the essence of the soul is reason and simple form, and to this extent one soul will differ in no respect from another essentially, but will differ according to form, for by character alone will it differ. But it is form alone. Whence it is evident that every soul, even though it is replete to the same degree with the same reasons, yet is allotted a form distinct from others, just as the solar form characterizes the solar soul, and another form another soul.

PHANES PRESS both publishes and distributes many fine books
which relate to the philosophical, religious and spiritual traditions
of the Western world. To obtain a copy of our current catalogue,
please write:

PHANES PRESS
PO BOX 6114
GRAND RAPIDS, MI 49516
USA